# Contemporary Issues
# In Education

*At the Interface*

Dr Robert Fisher
**Series Editor**

**Advisory Board**

Dr Margaret Sönser Breen
Professor Margaret Chatterjee
Dr Salwa Ghaly
Professor Michael Goodman
Professor Asa Kasher
Mr Christopher Macallister

Professor Diana Medlicott
Revd Stephen Morris
Professor John Parry
Dr David Seth Preston
Professor Bernie Warren
Revd Dr Kenneth Wilson, O.B.E

**Volume 22**

A volume in the *At The Interface* project
'The Idea of Education'

*Probing the Bounderies*

# Contemporary Issues In Education

Edited by

David Seth Preston

Amsterdam - New York, NY 2005

The paper on which this book is printed meets the requirements of "ISO 9706:1994, Information and documentation - Paper for documents - Requirements for permanence".

ISBN: 90-420-1684-1
©Editions Rodopi B.V., Amsterdam - New York, NY 2005
Printed in the Netherlands

# Contents

|  |  |  |
|---|---|---|
|  | Preface | ix |
| CHAPTER ONE | Revitalising Pedagogy? Teaching and Technology in the University Classroom | 1 |
|  | *Denton Anthony and Lars K. Hallström* |  |
| CHAPTER TWO | From Process to Product: Quality Audits and Instrumental Reason | 19 |
|  | *Gillian Howie* |  |
| CHAPTER THREE | Emergent Skills in Higher Education: The Quest for Emotion and Virtual University | 37 |
|  | *Luis Borges Gouveia* |  |
| CHAPTER FOUR | Myths and Realities of Higher Education as a Vehicle for Nation Building in Developing Countries: The Culture of the University and the New African Diaspora | 49 |
|  | *Seth A. Agbo* |  |
| CHAPTER FIVE | From 'Education' to 'Educability': The Changing Nature of the Research/Teaching Nexus in the Modern University | 71 |
|  | *Tom Claes* |  |
| CHAPTER SIX | Student Expectations: How Was It For You? | 89 |
|  | *Tony Tricker* |  |
| CHAPTER SEVEN | Let's Go Out and Learn | 101 |
|  | *Paramita Atmodiwirjo and Yandi Andri Yatmo* |  |
| CHAPTER EIGHT | The Hidden Presumptions of Commercially Derived Quality Management in Higher Education | 115 |
|  | *Trudi Cooper* |  |

| CHAPTER NINE | "A Plea for the Highlands of Scotland": University Reform in the Early Twentieth Century | 141 |

*Christine D. Myers*

| CHAPTER TEN | Funding Challenges for a South African University A Case Study | 159 |

*Herman Rhode and Kirti Menon*

| CHAPTER ELEVEN | The Problems Faced By Higher Education Institutions Because of the Constantly Changing Objectives, Sometimes Imposed Externally, Sometimes Self-Imposed | 171 |

*Frank McMahon*

| | Notes on Contributors | 187 |
| | Index | 191 |

# Welcome to an *At the Interface* Publication

By sharing insights and perspectives that are inter- and multi-disciplinary, *ATI* publications are both exploratory examinations of particular areas and issues, and rigorous inquiries into specific subjects. Books published in the series are enabling resources which encourage sustained and creative dialogue, becoming the future resource for further inquiries and research.

The *Idea of Education* cross-disciplinary research project aims to provide a vigorous forum for the examination of university and college education. Committed to the tradition of liberal education, the inherent value of the pursuit of learning and the principle that knowledge must be an end in itself, publications will examine the nature and aims of institutes of higher education, their guiding principles, practical functions, and role in society.

Themes examined in the series will include;

- what a university or college should be; where ideas of what a university or college is should come from; what higher education 'is'; what the aims of higher education should be
- the nature of education; the role of liberal arts education; 'instruction', 'training' and 'vocational training'; the 'usefulness' and 'value' of education; distance and open learning.
- the changing landscapes of education; 'students', 'pupils', 'learners' and 'customers'; 'lecturer', 'teacher', 'tutor', 'mentor'; student services; course review and evaluation; modularization
- the 'business' of the university - the rise of managerialism; intellectual capital and copyright; knowledge, research and teaching; the preservation and diffusion of knowledge
- external issues impacting on education: funding education; private sector involvement; Academic Audit; Research Assessment Exercise; QAA; Teaching Quality Assessment.
- internal issues impacting on education: key/transferable skills; access to education; life-long education; adult education; returning to learning
- the role of the university and college in society; the contexts of the university and college; the needs of society; reconceiving the place and work of the university and college.

Dr Robert Fisher
Inter-Disciplinary.Net
www.inter-disciplinary.net

# Preface

"regretting that in the old days..... lectures were more frequent ..... but now the time taken for lectures is being spent in meetings and discussions"
Chancellor of University of Paris 1213

Following the success of the first 'Idea of Education' conference held at Mansfield College Oxford in 2002 and the subsequent edited volume, there was much enthusiasm and interest in a second conference. This conference was held the following year at the same venue. I hope this edited book, the second volume of the 'Idea of Education' project series, provides the reader a fairly representative, coherent and cohesive statement of the 2003 conference. Perhaps my abiding memory will be of the above quote, provided by Frank McMahon our keynote speaker, and cited in his chapter in this book which demonstrates that some of the questions raised around education have been with us for a surprisingly long time. The third 'Idea of Education' conference is to be held in Prague in August 2004, and I hope the quality of the presentation and informal discussion meets the high standards set by the previous two conferences.

In Chapter One of this volume, Denton Anthony and Lars Hallström examine how the proliferation and common use of information and communication technologies impact student behaviour and learning. Using a case study they investigate interactive learning to determine whether students and teachers have differing expectations of technology-based learning. They conclude that the causal factors affecting learning are discipline dependent and that there is a fundamental difference between student and teacher expectations of what constitutes "participation" and interaction.

In Chapter Two Gillian Howie analyses how harmony exists between quality audit processes and the functional purpose of the higher education system to produce performance driven, social ends. Dr Howie suggest that the increased use of new technologies into higher education has modified not only what and how education is delivered but also provided a vehicle for the restructuring of the sector to meet these political ends. She claims that as a result of harmonisation, learning has become an exchangeable good, critical reason has been converted into instrumental reason and the aim of practical-virtue has been replaced by skills accumulation and credit transfer.

In Chapter Three Luis Borges Gouveia examines issues raised for Higher Education by the development of sophisticated tools and techniques congruent with the Informtion Society. In particular Dr Gouveia investigates how virtuality provides the opportunity to cope with erstwhile time and space constraints and to innovate both on practices and on what individuals need to know. Furthermore the cahpter discusses the skills that may emerge from adopting a virtual approach to higher education and its likely impact.

In Chapter Four Seth Agbo highlights a current dilemma in Africa created by lack of economic growth. Dr Agbo suggests that there are three main theories of African advancement: modernisation; human capital and dependency. He further suggests that all three owe much to the impact of the university and that they reflect the contradictions of socio-economic development. The chapter claims that the processes of higher education have not always resulted in development. The African university has resisted change as it strives to remain protected from external interference. As a result the artificial environment of the African university helps only to serve the interests of the former colonial powers.

In Chapter Five Tom Claes argues that traditionally the research/teaching nexus is seen as central to the modern university, and that recent change to the preferred type and mode of research that takes place has fundamental consequences for the identity of the 'modern university.' The chapter focuses mainly on the European level and on the policies and trends that have shaped the university landscape from the last decades of the 20th century onwards. He answers three interrelated, questions: what are the main characteristics of the new economic rationale for the university?; What are the emerging dominant types of university research that accompany this new rationale?; and How does this influence the research and teaching mission of the university? Dr Claes suggests that this modern university faces problems that threaten its traditional identity, which could very well lead to the end of the traditional university.

In Chapter Six Tony Tricker suggests that the student experience has become an significant element in the measurement of the quality of education, due to the current tendency to consider students in higher education as customers. Dr. Tricker first illustrates how student expectations have changed over the last thirty years and identifies the drivers for this change. The chapter then demonstrates how a web based interactive version of a 'Service Template,' can help in providing students with a closer approximation to the higher education experience they seek

In Chapter Seven Paramita Atmodiwirjo and Yandi Andri Yatmo discuss the supportive role physical setting plays in the learning process. In particular they use a case study to analyse the outdoor environment as a physical resource in architectural education. They demonstrate how, alongside the learning activities in the traditional design studio, learning activities in outdoor spaces can become a key element of the overall learning process

In Chapter Eight Trudi Cooper highlights how the use of commercially derived quality management techniques across the world has led to changes in the language used within higher education. In particular she utilises data from Australia to examine whether the presumption that business relationships can be applied to the context of higher education can be justified. Dr. Cooper suggests that application of business language to universities uncovers irresolvable contradictions, and that quality in higher education must be re-conceptualised to take account of differences between higher education and business.

In Chapter Nine Christine Myers outlines the work of Hugh Gunn, one of the leading proponents of reform in British education in the early twentieth century. Dr Myers examines Gunn's work on the Scottish university system which detailed the need for better distribution of universities in Britain. The chapter focuses primarily on what Gunn terms "A Plea for the Highlands of Scotland" and in particular Gunn's call to bilingual (Gaelic) education.

In Chapter Ten Herman Rhode and Kirti Menon suggest higher education across the world is suffering from diminishing resources, and as a result universities are broadening access and improving how they manage knowledge strategically. Currently, higher education in South Africa is being restructured in order to shift the system from an apartheid-defined landscape to one that is equitable, responsive and accessible. In this chapter the authors examine current South African policies with a view to exposing the intended and unintended consequences of these for the University of the North. A case is presented for an alternative costing model for use in such environments.

In Chapter Eleven Frank McMahon highlights how the objectives that universities and other higher education institutions try to achieve are changing. Dr McMahon demonstrates that as a result a multiplicity of objectives has emerged. He suggests that both the multiplicity of these new objectives and their inconsistency create problems for universities that try to achieve them. The chapter argues that global trends in higher education are adding to the problems facing university leaders and posits possible solutions.

I am grateful to all the contributors and the Series Editor Rob Fisher for being so helpful in answering my many queries. In addition I owe an enormous debt to Stephanie Bartlett for her recommendations and practical skills in formatting, editing, proofreading and all manner of technological talents.

Since the first volume of 'The Idea of Education' appeared, Middlesbrough has after 128 years actually won a trophy, the Carling Cup. I would like to thank the whole Club for a terrific season and in particular for providing supporters like me with a unique afternoon in Cardiff that we will never forget. For that alone I dedicate this book to them.

> For
> Middlesbrough Football Club
>
> Dr D.S. Preston
> London
> Email: David-Preston@blueyonder.co.uk
> May 2004

# CHAPTER ONE

## Revitalising Pedagogy? Teaching and Technology in the University Classroom

*Denton Anthony and Lars K. Hallström*

**Abstract**
 As computing technologies and software such as Microsoft PowerPoint have become increasingly available to university faculty, the question is raised as to how these technologies affect student behaviour and learning. This study develops a predictive model that investigates the technology-relevant factors that contribute to interactive learning. Based on a survey of undergraduate students at St. Francis Xavier University, we test the hypothesis that students and faculty come into the classroom setting with existing models for the roles and purposes of technology and technology use. We note that these models may not, however, coincide, leading to frustration with the teaching/learning experience. We find that there are a number of causal factors present that affect interactive learning, but these factors do differ between disciplines. Additionally, we find that student models of what constitutes 'participation' and interaction tend to be very low, resulting in additional sources of tension between faculty and student expectations.

Key words: technology; interactive learning; asynchronous learning; Microsoft PowerPoint; student participation; pedagogy.

## 1. Introduction

 From the first time a teacher used a sharp rock or stick to illustrate a concept or to demonstrate a computation, technology has been an integral part of the educational experience. However, while the use of in-class technology remained largely constant for several centuries, relying on the use of chalkboards, and later overheads, to present course materials, the past few decades have seen a dramatic shift in the role and nature of technology. With the rise of the personal computer, the Internet and an increasingly computer-savvy student population, faculty are faced with a plurality of technological options when teaching. At the same time, student expectations of faculty, access to course materials, in-class participation and technology usage are also changing, creating a learning environment in the lecture hall that can be highly beneficial for both student and instructor. However, these technological changes and demands can also create possible conflicts, particularly when faculty and student expectations and usage of technology do not coincide, whether for personal, pedagogical, or experiential reasons.

As a result of the increasing availability of different technologies and the shift in demand for asynchronous learning environments from students, there is an increasing awareness of the import of technological changes for pedagogical practices[1]. As noted by Clawson, Deen, and Oxley[2], "the initial research into the pedagogical effectiveness of these merging technologies suggests there are many ways in which they might be useful." Technological innovations can foster student participation (although not necessarily in the lecture hall), increase comprehension, and provide students with a greater degree of autonomy with course materials.

In this study, while we seek to contribute to this growing literature, we take a slightly different starting point. Given the assumption that technology is used by both students and faculty as a result of some perceived set of benefits, we examine student opinion, demographic variables and larger narratives of technology in the educational process as the first stages of a larger investigation. Specifically, we begin from one possible faculty perspective toward the use of technology - to transmit data and facilitate learning, with possible complementary goals of organisation and even in-class participation. Based upon our own experiences using computing technology in the lecture hall, we then proceed to the general hypothesis driving this research: Both students and faculty enter the classroom with pre-formed assumptions (or models) of the purposes for technology and its use in the course. However, we hypothesise that these models often do not coincide, and may in some cases not even be compatible. This can result in both student and faculty dissatisfaction with the educational experience, and may also affect the learning models being developed by students. As we noted in an earlier paper[3], "the changing (technological) environment of post-secondary education...may also be contributing to a growing gap between the teaching objectives of faculty and the learning objectives (and behaviours) of students." At a more operational level, we test two additional hypotheses: (1) Students who are comfortable with computing technology and have higher levels of exposure to technology use in the educational context will view computing technology use at the university level more favourably than those with lesser levels of comfort and exposure; (2) Measures of attitudes and behaviours that favour interactive learning will be higher in students of higher economic status with previous exposure to computing technology and interactive teaching methods.

As the first stage of a multi-stage and year project, this study is built around the use of student-based focus groups and a 32-question survey to meet four primary goals. These goals are to: (1) Uncover student perceptions of the role technology should (and does) play in the lecture hall; (2) Identify factors that predict positive evaluations of technology use;

(3) Determine the factors and the role technology plays in creating an interactive learning forum; and (4) Draw tentative conclusions for the creation of more compatible models of effective technology use. It is our hope that not only can this line of research assist the effective use of computing technology in university education, but also inform a larger and still evolving discourse surrounding changes to student culture, the role of the university as an institution of higher learning and how both students and faculty address the learning process.

At a practical level, this study stems not only from our use of PowerPoint in teaching political science and business, but also from our realisation that using such technologies appeared to trigger student learning behaviours that were not consistent with our expectations. More specifically, we became concerned that while we both use a highly interactive and participatory teaching style, using PowerPoint (even when specifically intended to generate student participation) often triggered largely passive responses. Simply put, students focus on copying PowerPoint slides and pay limited attention to the spoken content of the course, whether in lecture or discussion format. It was this consistent behaviour in both disciplines that leads to the realisation that not only must there be some underlying cause or value set for this activity worthy of investigation, but also that there is a gap or disparity between how we, as instructors, design and implement the use of such technology, and the ways that students interpret that design and act upon that interpretation.

## 2. Research Design and Methods

We chose to examine the role and effects of PowerPoint as an operational form of in-class technology for three reasons:

1) As a medium that essentially mimics the presentation of course materials in traditional formats such as overhead transparencies, MS PowerPoint can be used by both students and faculty as what Thomson identifies as a Traditional Synchronous Form. However, the combination of a common and easily available electronic format, accessibility via the Web and the ability to link to and create highly interactive, web-enhanced presentations make PowerPoint a flexible tool for delivery of course content[4];
2) MS PowerPoint can resolve some common practical issues in teaching, including organisation of lecture or class content, legibility and visual aids for students;
3) MS PowerPoint has been used, in slightly different ways, by both authors at St. Francis Xavier University since 2001. This provides an excellent opportunity to examine not only student perspectives, but to compare demographic, behavioural and attitudinal responses between undergraduate students in political science and

management. Although we recognise that there are many other forms of technology available to this line of research, we feel that PowerPoint is a technology option that, while apparently simple in both its use and effects, also embodies the underlying tensions between faculty and student models of technology usage[5].

There was a two-stage research design developed for this project. The initial stage consisted of collecting data from self-selecting focus groups comprised of first and second year undergraduate students from the academic disciplines of business and political science. This exploratory stage was followed by quantitative analysis of a survey using a different sample group, consisting again of undergraduate students primarily in their first and second years of post secondary education.

The initial stage was exploratory in nature as we felt this approach provided several advantages. Following Bellenger, Bernhardt and Goldstuker, the initial use of focus groups were used to generate hypotheses that could be further tested quantitatively, to generate information that may be useful in generating a survey questionnaire, and to help interpret previously obtained quantitative results from our review of literature[6]. The informal atmosphere of the focus groups allowed participants an environment where they could openly contribute and feel free to engage in dialogue with their fellow students. We strongly felt that the group interaction that occurred in this type of setting would act to stimulate new ideas and thoughts amongst group members. Group and peer pressure were not a concern given the nature of the subject matter.

Six focus groups were conducted consisting of between four and seven participants, taken from a sample of the researchers' classes. Two groups were comprised of only business students, two groups of only political science students and two groups of combined students. Each group was moderated by a neutral moderator to avoid any additional constraining factors. Each focus group session was video taped for further analysis as moderators were instructed not to take notes in an attempt not to guide group discussions in inadvertent ways.[7] [8] Five simple research questions were chosen to guide the focus group discussions:

1) How do these students view the purpose and use of PowerPoint in the lecture hall, and why?
2) How do students actually use PowerPoint presentations, both in the lecture hall, and out?
3) Do student models of technology coincide with those of the faculty involved?
4) Are there methods of improving learning by generating compatible models?

5) What effects (negative and positive) does the use of PowerPoint have upon student models of learning?

One year later, stage two of the study was carried out with a new sample group. This portion of research was greatly enhanced by the focus group discussions. The researchers developed a 32-question, structured questionnaire to:

1) Uncover students perceptions on the role technology should play in the classroom.
2) Identify any factors that may predict positive student evaluations of technology in the classroom.
3) Determine the role technology plays increasing an interactive forum within the classroom.
4) Determine effective methods of learning by generating compatible student and professor models.

The survey was administered to two sections of an introductory political science course and two sections of a second year introductory marketing course (n=134). Survey participants included both genders, majors from a wide range of academic disciplines and students within their first three years of university study. There were significantly more males (66%) to females (33%) in our sample. Over 93% of the respondents were between the ages of 17-22. In terms of ethnicity, our sample was predominately Caucasian (Caucasian - 89.6%, Asian - 3%, African - 3%, Other –3%, Aboriginal Canadian - 0.7%).

In order to simplify the processing of the data, the questions were of a closed type with multiple-choice selections, scaling and ranking questions, including the use of an itemised ratings scale. SPSS was used to code and enter the raw data that enabled the generation and analyses of descriptive statistics. In addition, we used multivariate regression analysis to test our models of student evaluation of technology and interactive participation against our independent variables.

## 3. Findings
A. Stage One - Focus Groups

The group discussions raised many student suggestions, concerns and benefits. Overall, students favour the use of PowerPoint in the classroom, so much so that one student declared that students are becoming 'addicted to PowerPoint.' Other students felt that the use of PowerPoint did not encourage participation (using an interactive model of questions and fill-in the blanks), rather the presentation merely provided them with something to look at, namely 'eye candy.'

Students also raised many concerns about the use of PowerPoint by faculty members. Some students were of the opinion that PowerPoint fosters laziness in students and in faculty. A common concern was the lack of uniformity of use by faculty across the university. However, this point was also contradicted as many students said that they expected some variation in use from subject to subject, and across different disciplines.

PowerPoint presentations that were made available to students outside of the classroom appeared to provide students with a number of benefits. Perceived benefits cited by students include providing organisation to facilitate studying, improving interest in the subject matter, creating an alternate focus due to less note-taking and saving time because 'simpler is (supposedly) better.' One very surprising benefit raised by some students was that the use of PowerPoint fosters technology skills that are more important than listening and note-taking skills[9].

B. Stage Two - Survey Data

To uncover students' perceptions on the role technology should play in the classroom, we built upon the work of stage one of this research project. A series of questions relating to students' attitudes about technology, and their exposure to technology prior and during their brief university career were put forward in the survey. Student responses were consistent with the stage one findings. Access to class lecture material outside of the classroom was cited as a positive. This is consistent with literature by Thomson in his description of synchronous and asynchronous learning[10]. The major drawback to PowerPoint use cited by the students was something that is usually beyond the control of the professor: technology failure. However the next 'worst' element of PowerPoint as identified by the students was how it was actually used. Students did not look favourably upon faculty who 'read' their slides. Additional results are summarised in Tables 1 and 2.

**Table 1. Positive Elements of PowerPoint Use**

| Element of PowerPoint | Percentage of Students Reporting |
|---|---|
| Legibility | .7 |
| Organisation | 6.7 |
| Access outside of classroom | 29.6 |
| Interesting Visuals | 20.7 |
| All of the Above | 40.7 |

n=134

**Table 2. Negative Elements of PowerPoint Use**

| Element of PowerPoint | Percentage of Students Reporting |
|---|---|
| Too Much Information | 8.1 |
| Too many slides in time period | 10.4 |
| Trying to copy by hand | 16.3 |
| Faculty who 'read' slides | 27.4 |
| Technology does not work | 36.3 |

n= 134

C. Predicting Positive Student Evaluations of Technology Use

To identify what predicts positive student evaluations of computing technology, we analysed responses that allowed the students to assess their professors' ability and use of PowerPoint. A separate regression analysis was conducted using student assessment of technology as the dependent variable and a series of independent variables grouped in four student-based categories: primary computing ability, exposure to technology prior to and during university, demographic factors and student characteristics.

**Table 3. Predictors of Positive Student Evaluations of Technology in the Classroom**

|  | Unstandardised Coefficients | Standard Errors | Standard Coefficients | Significance |
|---|---|---|---|---|
| ***Computing Ability:*** | | | | |
| Primary Ability | .384 | .177 | .204 | .032 |
| PC Ownership | -1.066 | .865 | -.001 | .990 |
| ***Exposure to Technology:*** | | | | |
| Pre-University Exposure | -.189 | .120 | .143 | .117 |
| University Exposure | .229 | .112 | .225 | .042 |
| ***Demographics:*** | | | | |
| Age | -1.030 | .395 | -.003 | .979 |
| Family Income | .238 | .153 | .146 | .123 |
| Gender | -.729 | .431 | -.155 | .094 |
| ***Student Characteristics:*** | | | | |
| Employment | -.130 | .257 | -.046 | .616 |
| Grade Point Average | -.235 | .247 | -.092 | .344 |
| Semesters in University | .140 | .227 | .076 | .537 |

Dependent Variable: Student Evaluation

Significant effects were found in two of these independent variables. Students' exposure to technology while at university and their primary computing ability, were significant predictors of positive student evaluations of technology in the classroom. Using cross-tabulation, it was discovered that business students were more exposed to PowerPoint in their classrooms than their political science counterpoints. Similarly, business students also assessed their ability to use computing technology as higher than political science students (with means of 2.83/4.0 and 2.19/4.0 respectively. These differences are statistically significant, and point to the importance of recognising disciplinary factors when considering the effects of technology. However, despite these differences, it is important to note that on the whole, students are highly adept at using certain aspects of computing technology for basic tasks and communication, with a number indicating the ability to use computers beyond simple tasks.

Students were asked to assess their primary ability with computing software. Nearly 60% of the students responded to one of two categories of email/web surfing and word processing/spreadsheets. One-third of the students evaluated their primary computing ability as high which included data basing and web site design along with the previously mentioned two categories. This finding suggests that stronger computing ability as indicated by our sample will lead to positive student evaluations of technology in the classroom. Students are exposed to technology in many aspects of their lives, and a positive evaluation leads us to suggest that students who score their own computing ability as high favour technology being used in the classroom. It was further suggested in stage one group discussions that technical skills associated with today's learning environment, are more valuable than traditional pedagogical values of listening and note-taking. The researchers were somewhat surprised by this finding, yet it was consistent of the divide between faculty and student values in terms of pedagogy. It is our view that technology should act as a support for pedagogy and not a replacement for listening and communication skills that are so valuable in any learning environment.

D. Technology and Interactive Participation

In order to understand the role technology plays in creating an active forum within the classroom, the researchers developed another model based on data collected from survey results. The model was designed to test for factors that would predict active learning behaviours beyond the control of the researchers. More specifically, we test the hypothesis (see above) that interactive student behaviours are a function of the exposure to interactive teaching methods, financial resources and the educational status of the student.[11]

Three separate multivariate regressions were completed - a composite using the entire sample, one for business students (n= 55) and a final analysis for political science students (n=79). The dependent variable consisted of a number of posts intended to measure interactive learning. All models consisted of the same four categories of independent variables identified previously.

The regression analysis produced some very intriguing results (see Table 4). The composite model showed exposure to technology prior to university to be a significant indicator for predicting students' levels of interactive learning ($p = .015$). The number of semesters of post-secondary education completed also proved to be a significant indicator as well ($p = .046$). This finding is somewhat consistent with our hypothesis that interactive participation is a function of the educational status of the student. However, grade point average proved not to be a significant factor in predicting high or low levels of interactive learning.

**Table 4. Technology's role in creating an Interactive Forum – *All Students***

|  | Unstandardised Coefficients | Standard Errors | Standard Coefficients | Significance |
|---|---|---|---|---|
| ***Computing Ability:*** | | | | |
| Primary Ability | .196 | .185 | .097 | .292 |
| PC Ownership | .941 | .885 | .091 | .290 |
| ***Exposure to Technology:*** | | | | |
| Pre-University Exposure | .306 | .124 | .217 | .015 |
| University Exposure | 1.590 | .116 | .015 | .891 |
| Student Evaluation | -.5.567 | .097 | -.052 | .567 |
| ***Demographics:*** | | | | |
| Age | -.398 | .404 | -.102 | .328 |
| Family Income | .375 | .215 | .215 | .020 |
| Gender | .160 | .447 | .032 | .720 |
| ***Student Characteristics:*** | | | | |
| Employment Variable | .512 | .263 | .170 | .055 |
| Grade Point Average | -.375 | .254 | -.138 | .142 |
| Semesters in University | .470 | .232 | .237 | .046 |

Dependent Variable: Interactive Participation

**Table 5. Technology's role in creating an Interactive Forum –** *Business Students*

| | Unstandardised Coefficients | Standard Errors | Standard Coefficients | Significance |
|---|---|---|---|---|
| ***Computing Ability:*** | | | | |
| Primary Ability | .134 | .328 | .067 | .687 |
| PC Ownership | 3.334 | 1.908 | .284 | .089 |
| ***Exposure to Technology:*** | | | | |
| Pre-University Exposure | .156 | .173 | .134 | .373 |
| University Exposure | .287 | .267 | .163 | .289 |
| Student Evaluation | -.115 | .166 | -.106 | .491 |
| ***Demographics:*** | | | | |
| Age | -.635 | .729 | -.157 | .389 |
| Family Income | .660 | .278 | .215 | .023 |
| Gender | 3.083 | .752 | .386 | .968 |
| ***Student Characteristics:*** | | | | |
| Employment Variable | -.811 | .667 | -.178 | .232 |
| Grade Point Average | -.759 | .254 | -.318 | .068 |
| Semesters in University | .972 | .404 | .320 | .070 |

Dependent Variable: Interactive Participation

Our hypothesis that interactive learning is a function of financial resources proved to be correct (p = .023). The basic assumption here is that increased financial resources will lead to increased opportunities for using different computing technologies. In separating the two groups based on academic discipline, the educational status of the student (numbers of semesters), no longer was as significant as expected. Business students who had higher overall levels of participation were for the most part enrolled in university for a longer period of time. There is the assumption that comfort levels with professors and fellow students may be a cause of this. The hypothesis that interactive learning is a function of family resources again was proven to be significant with business students in the regression analysis (see Table 6).

The only independent variable that was significant to interactive participation for political science students was employment history. This finding was not directly forecasted. However, we believe that this result may be associated with the students' use of a computer in their employment (see Table 6).

**Table 6. Technology's role in creating an Interactive Forum – *Political Science***

|  | Unstandardised Coefficients | Standard Errors | Standard Coefficients | Significance |
|---|---|---|---|---|
| ***Computing Ability:*** | | | | |
| Primary Ability | 4.008 | .256 | .021 | .880 |
| PC Ownership | .424 | 1.057 | .049 | .690 |
| ***Exposure to Technology:*** | | | | |
| Pre-University Exposure | .274 | .208 | .163 | .192 |
| University Exposure | -.224 | .158 | -.192 | .161 |
| Student Evaluation | 1.781 | .122 | .018 | .884 |
| ***Demographics:*** | | | | |
| Age | .179 | .564 | .052 | .752 |
| Family Income | .276 | .209 | .174 | .193 |
| Gender | .331 | .568 | .074 | .563 |
| ***Student Characteristics:*** | | | | |
| Employment Variable | .790 | .286 | .334 | .007 |
| Grade Point Average | -.494 | .358 | -.184 | .173 |
| Semesters in University | .133 | .325 | .065 | .684 |

Dependent Variable: Interactive Participation

## 4. Implications and Concluding Comments

The findings noted above point to a number of possible conclusions and implications to be considered in the integration of MS PowerPoint into undergraduate classes. The obvious differences in the causal relationships between business and political science students point to the importance of considering not only the target audience, but also the reasons behind variation between major streams. Although political science and business students at St. Francis Xavier University do demonstrate differences in key areas such as income, employment and the presentation of course materials (it is rare for first and second year political science courses to hinge on case studies), there is a more important factor to recognise in these findings. While we, as faculty, are generally concerned with maintaining the rigour of our respective disciplines and providing an informative and participatory learning environment, these provisions need not lead to the interactive learning environment that many of us hope to achieve. While there is little doubt that thoughtful and organised attempts to foster interactive learning, participation and student use of MS PowerPoint in a way that coincides with, or is at least compatible with, instructor intent, the findings presented here indicate an additional problem. As demonstrated by the multivariate regression analyses of both political science and business students as separate groups, the only significant predictors of interactive attitudes and behaviours (employment and income respectively) are entirely independent of the educational experience.

This finding raises an entire set of important questions that simply cannot be addressed here, but that should be considered within the larger context of both 'who participates' and 'why.' When treated as a single sample, the first and second year students used in this study have three statistically significant predictors for interactive learning: their semester of education, income and prior exposure. However, when divided by discipline, the importance of employment and family income point to the possibility of student attitudes and behaviours that stem from sociological factors affected by financial status. Such factors include a possible sense of entitlement or privileged access to in-class participation, a class-based sense of superiority (or inferiority) that can induce or limit participation, and particularly for business students, a sense that higher family income may indicate more or qualitatively better 'knowledge' of management and marketing practices. Obviously, while the presence and effects of these potential factors cannot be addressed here, it is important to note that class and financially based factors, while well beyond any form of faculty or administrative control, should be considered when designing and implementing technology use and participatory exercises. In particular, while it may not be possible to 'control' income and employment-based effects, faculty should, perhaps, be aware of the way such factors might bias discussions, or even alienate other students.

A second important factor stemming from these results lies in the perceptions of both business and political science students about not only what constitutes 'participation' but also what is considered an acceptable or reasonable frequency of participation in a class that includes a separate, and often substantial, participation grade.[12] While participants in the 2002 focus groups indicated that many students felt that they should not be pressured or 'forced' to talk or participate in-class if they do not wish to, the survey findings indicated that many students view participation in the lecture hall as positive or beneficial. In both political science and business classes, a substantial portion of students feel that students should, in fact, participate in class, yet the self-assessment of frequency of participation points to a disparity between student opinion and actual participatory activity, driven partially by disciplinary differences.

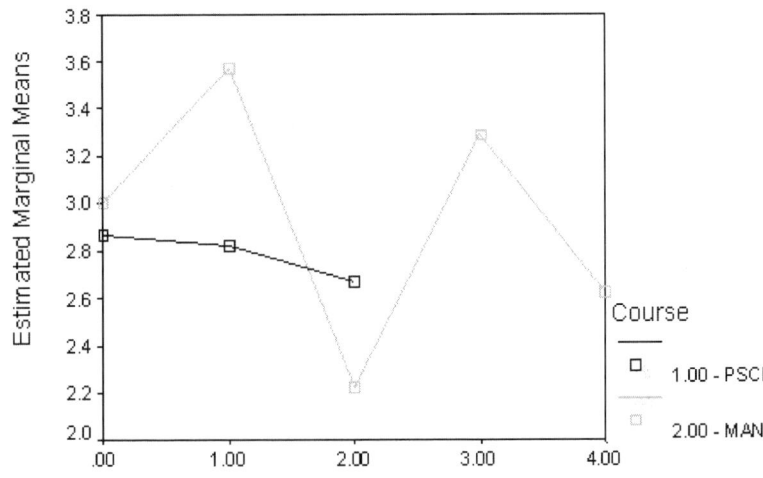

**Frequency of Participation**

Non-estimable means are not plotted

**Figure 1. Should Students Participate?**

More specifically, although most students surveyed for this study felt that students should participate (over 53%) the actual levels of student participation are really quite low, with political science students demonstrating significantly lower frequencies than students enrolled in the business classes. In fact, no students from the political science classes indicated that they participated more than once or twice a month in any of their classes. In contrast, just over sixty-seven percent of students enrolled in business indicated that they participate at least every week, and even every class. There are a number of explanations for this difference, including variations in the content, delivery and format of course materials between the social sciences and business. Although class participation and discussions are often a component of courses in the social sciences, they may differ a great deal from classes in business that are built around a core or combination of case studies and student involvement. This is supported by the significant difference between student assessments of whether faculty encourage student participation - students from the business sample indicated that their instructors did encourage such activity, while the political science sample was less positive. A third and related explanation involves factors mentioned above - the effects of employment and income on attitudinal factors not measured by this survey such as entitlement or a 'right' to participate and be involved in class discussions. Student perceptions of when they should participate, and how, often vary considerably, and students can have difficulty separating rhetorical from non-rhetorical questions. Demographic variables, along with intangibles such as comfort speaking in public[13] and opinions on a student's role, can interact with different teaching styles and content to affect participation levels.

These effects are made apparent in Figure 1 (above). Although it was expected that students who felt that they should participate in class would actually be the respondents with higher levels of participation, this does not hold true. The political science students are quite consistent, with low frequencies of participation balanced by a moderate expectation of participation (hovering around 2.8/5.0), but business students showed considerable variation that is neither consistent nor expected. Of this sample, students who self-assessed their participation to be high actually had the second lowest assessment of whether they *should* participate, an assessment lower than students who claimed to participate only a handful of time per term! At the other end of the scale, business students who indicated most strongly that students should participate in class averaged participation only one or two times per term, a result certainly not consistent with what we, as faculty would expect.

However, it is in this context of the expectations of faculty, and those of students, that the concluding comments of this paper shall be made. Obviously, the 'gap' between student expectation of whether they should participate, and the degree that the actually do participate, is only a gap from one perspective. It is entirely possible that the students sampled do, in fact, view participating in the lecture hall three or four times as year as 'acceptable' - if not more so. What this points to, specifically within the context of interactive learning, is the importance of recognising and articulating not only our expectations of student activity, but to obtain, and if necessary, 'modify' student beliefs surrounding their role in the lecture hall. Although this can perhaps be achieved through opening an honest and frank dialogue with students about what 'in-class participation' means, it also involves the recognition by faculty that as we use certain types of technology, such as MS PowerPoint, these technologies can reinforce certain assumptions, and consequentially behaviours, of students in the lecture hall.

In conclusion, this study has demonstrated some of the larger empirical trends and causal relationships that exist between technology, technology use and student activity in post-secondary education. However, it is also an attempt to place these relationships within a larger pedagogical context of interactive learning, and to explore the ways that computer technologies such as MS PowerPoint can both contribute to, and detract from, the undergraduate learning experience. Ultimately, these admittedly limited studies point to numerous inconsistencies and insecurities on the part of students when questioned about technology. Almost all see computing technologies in the lecture hall such as websites, PowerPoint presentations and communications technology as positive, but when pressed to explain how and why, have difficulty doing so. Similarly, student understanding of what constitutes 'active learning' and in-class participation tend to be low, but a substantial portion of students sampled in our research felt that students should participate. Not only might this become a possible source of tension or frustration between students and faculty (students feel they ARE participating, but faculty press for more), but it also points to a larger set of issues surrounding the role of post-secondary education, the student as 'customer' and the commodification of 'knowledge' embodied in the fetishised status of on-line PowerPoint presentations.

# Notes

[1] Michael J. Thomson, "Technology Levels and Teaching American Government," Annual Meeting of the American Political Science Association, (2002) Boston, MA.

[2] Rosealee A. Clawson, Rebecca E. Deen, and Zoe M. Oxley. "On-Line Discussions Across Three Universities: Student Participation and Pedagogy," PS: Political Science & Politics 35, 4 (2002):712-717.

[3] Denton Anthony and Lars K. Hallström, "Teaching Objectives and Microsoft PowerPoint: Student Evaluations of Technology," in Atlantic Universities Teaching Showcase 2002, eds. Andrew Robb and Denise Nevo (Halifax: Mount Saint Vincent University, 2002), 93-105.

[4] Thomson.

[5] Although it has been suggested that Microsoft PowerPoint is not technology we remain convinced that not only is PowerPoint a valid operational use of computing technology, its application exceeds the suggestions of DVDs or videos. This is due to PowerPoint's in-class reliance on involvement from (at a minimum) faculty, and hopefully students. DVDs or video present a highly uni-linear flow of data, and while PowerPoint can certainly do the same, it does require activity from the instructor.

[6] D. Bellenger, K.L. Bernhardt, and J.L. Goldstucker, "Qualitative

Research in Marketing," in Monograph Series No.3, (Chicago: American Marketing Association, 1976), 145-159.

[7] Keith Middlemas. Orchestrating Europe: The Informal Politics of the European Union 1973-1995. (London: Fontana Press, 1995).

[8] Michael Brenner et al., The Research Interview: Uses and Approaches (London: Harcourt Brace Janovich, 1985).

[9] Anthony and Hallström.

[10] Thomson.

[11] A comparison of R-squares also reinforces the suitability of our models, and the importance of recognizing disciplinary differences. The R-square for the regression conducted with all students was .234, indicating substantial explanatory power of the model. However, when political science and business students are compared (with R-squares of .188 and .296 respectively) what emerges is a model that is better suited to business students. This indicates that there are exogenous factors that affect interactive learning for political science students. These might include the range and diversity of coursework and faculty that political science students are exposed to, their confidence levels, and the possibility of discipline-specific teaching styles.

[12] Both authors require students to participate orally in classes.

[13] Although over ninety percent of respondents indicated they were comfortable participating in class, this figure may be inaccurate.

## Bibliography

Anthony, Denton and Lars K. Hallström. "Teaching Objectives and Microsoft PowerPoint." In *Atlantic Universities' Teaching Showcase 2002*, edited by Andrew Robb and Denise Nevo, 93-105. Halifax: Mount Saint Vincent University, 2002.

Bellenger, D., K.L. Bernhardt, and J.L. Goldstucker. "Qualitative Research in Marketing." *Monograph Series* No.3. Chicago: American Marketing Association. (1976): 145-159.

Brenner, Michael, Jennifer Brown, and David Canter. *The Research Interview: Uses and Approaches*. London: Harcourt Brace Janovich. 1985.

Clawson, Rosealee A., Rebecca E. Deen, and Zoe M. Oxley. "On-Line Discussions Across Three Universities: Student Participation and Pedagogy." *PS: Political Science & Politics* 35, 4 (2002): 712-717.

Middlemas, Keith. *Orchestrating Europe: The Informal Politics of the European Union 1973-1995*. London: Fontana Press, 1995.

Thomson, J Michael. "Technology Levels and Teaching American Government". *Annual Meeting of the American Political Science Association.* (2002) Boston, MA.

# CHAPTER TWO

## From Process to Product: Quality Audits and Instrumental Reason

### Gillian Howie

**Abstract**

This paper investigates how quality audit processes harmonise the functional purpose of the higher education system with particular, performance driven, social ends. I suggest that the introduction of new technologies into higher education has modified not only the mode and content of delivery but also facilitated the restructuring of the sector to meet these political ends. I claim that as a result of harmonisation, learning has been transformed into an exchangeable good, critical reason has been converted into instrumental reason and the aim of practical-virtue replaced by skills accumulation and credit transfer.

Keywords: quality audits; performativity; Lyotard; Adorno; instrumental reason; reflection; exchange; technology; markets.

Contemporary arguments concerning the aim of higher education tend to re-enact controversies that have been an integral part of the history of philosophical disputes, from Plato onwards. The history of philosophy is littered with disagreements between civic legislators and spiritual directors, between those who focused on scientific and technological knowledge and those who wished to develop aesthetic sensibility or social sentiment. According to Aristotle, educational policy should be determined after a decision as to whether the citizen is interested primarily in a life of *theoria*, a life directed to eternal truths, or a life of practice-oriented virtue, *praxis*. Practical reason, which serves virtue and political deliberation, is found in well-formed habits of perception, emotion, and action and requires the development of specific sorts of abilities. That said, the life of *theoria* and the life of practical virtue are both essentially directed to the good of *eudaimonia*. To possess *eudaimonia* is to have a life that is objectively desirable and, thereby, to achieve the most worthwhile conditions available to humans.[1] The idea of an educational policy specifically modified to facilitate practice-oriented virtue seems echoed in recent discussions about the practical purpose of higher education. Indeed, insofar as the idea of *eudaimonia* overlaps with the modern idea of happiness we can see how controversies circle disagreements about how to translate 'the highest good' in terms of doing and living well. As we attempt to pick our way through the fragments of an inherited moral system, it is worth remembering that within the Aristotelian scheme, the good life cannot be specified outside the moral life and the moral life cannot be reduced to the quantification of pleasure.

Educational policy and philosophical analysis are inseparable, and it is unsurprising that at no time have universities been restricted to pure abstract learning. The University of Salerno in Italy, the earliest of European universities according to Alfred Whitehead, was devoted to medicine, and a college was founded at Cambridge, England, in 1316 for the special purpose of providing "clerks for the King's service."[2] Although oriented to the practical life, the primary reason for the existence of universities cannot be found in the simple transmission of knowledge, as this function could always be performed more cheaply elsewhere. Indeed, so far as the mere imparting of information is concerned, continues Whitehead, no university has had any justification for existence since the popularisation of printing in the fifteenth century. Even when directed to the practical life, universities have always reached beyond the simple transmission of information, attempting to preserve the connection between knowledge and zest for life, "by uniting young and old in the imaginative consideration of learning." It is almost a truism to suggest that education has a practical value: education is useful because understanding is useful.[3]

Whitehead concludes his commentary on the function of the university by focusing rather presciently on, what he describes as, "the problem of problems," how to provide the conditions for a learned and imaginative life to ever increasing numbers of students requesting ever diverse activities. Also considering the function of the university, but writing after the first major expansion of higher education, Jean-Francis Lyotard warns that higher education has become a subsystem of the social system, with the same performativity criterion applied to its problems as found elsewhere. In consequence, the function of the university has shifted and can be judged according to how it contributes to the most efficient performance of the social system. The dual-streamed practical function of higher education has collapsed into a solitary functional end: a contribution to the internal cohesion and increased performativity of the social world. The idea of usefulness is thus swallowed up into the idea of utility, defined in relation to efficient production.

While he investigates the impact of this performativity criterion on what is transmitted as knowledge within the educational context, Lyotard also alerts us to a new role attributed to higher education, concomitant with its functional end; that of job retraining and continuing education. I investigate elsewhere how performance criteria affect knowledge content and here wish to pursue the idea that the ends of the higher education system have been collapsed into ends determined from outside the sector. 4 Lyotard believes that aside from (research) universities, in departments or institutions with a professional orientation, knowledge and information will no longer be transmitted to young people entering the workforce, rather it will be served 'à la carte' to adults who are already working, or expect to be working - for the sole purpose of improving their skills and chances of promotion. Even if it were the case that the preponderance of the performance criterion sounded the death knell for the age of the professor - because a professor is no more competent than memory bank networks in transmitting established knowledge - this would not, in itself, bring into question either the contribution of the university to the social end, or the end itself.[5] Lyotard's pessimistic suggestion is that the moral life and the good life have been prised apart so successfully that the good life can only be defined in terms associated with performance: effectiveness; utility; and efficiency. An attempt to define political or social ends in terms of the good life will thus merely transmit performance criteria.

One can detect three main ways in which the university in the United Kingdom is being enjoined to contribute to the performance of the social system. Firstly, more focused research and concentrated teaching packages are supposedly required to support high technological and biotechnological industries, purportedly the mainstay of the new 'knowledge economy.' Secondly, by ensuring that education provision is flexible and responsive to business needs, higher education, alongside the further education sector, is asked to facilitate continuous and rapid retraining and reskilling of the workforce. Finally, the education sector is encouraged to recognise its global attractiveness and thus contribute to the wealth of the nation. Educationalists are struggling to interpret the life of practical virtue within a fragmentary moral scheme, where only the utilitarian identification of the good life with pleasure seems to make sense and practical utility is judged to be that which adds to individual, and thus aggregated, social capital.

Disharmony between functional ends, limited self-interest and general welfare, is smoothed out, according to Adam Smith, by an invisible hand, which coordinates human actions in such a way that behaviour promoting one will simultaneously promote the other.[6] The more recent 'human capital theory' mirrors the assumption that an increased quantification of individual capital will lead to greater economic performance. It is my contention that financial imperatives and interdicts have been blended with directives from the quality assurance agency so that the ends of higher education have been brought into harmony with particular political ends, thus ensuring the identity of deliverable interest between the individual, institution and economy. Harmonisation of ends has required the commercialisation of the higher education sector and commercialisation rests upon the principle that there is an exchangeable product, of which there can be multiple copies, distributable to numerous, yet already presupposed, recipients. On the other hand, if the proper function of the university is the imaginative acquisition of knowledge for a life of practical-virtue, it is also the case that imagination cannot be measured "by the yard or weighed by the pound; the learned and imaginative life is not an article of commerce." The problem, as indicated earlier by Whitehead, is not that there is a social good available to an increasing number of recipients; it is that education has become a product available *in principle* to a plurality of recipients: an article of commerce. The 'hidden' hand has not only introduced a culture of performativity, which itself has a menacing psychological impact on those who are managed accordingly, or are conduits for such judgments, but has also, concurrently, standardised the educational good and so has modified a (learning) process into a product, which can be exchanged in the global market.

The 'self-regulating market mechanism,' was seen by Smith, not as a means of achieving a static distribution of resources, but rather as a dynamic means of widening markets, promoting growth and developing the division of labour. Through the division of labour, diverse abilities and performance of diverse tasks could be made to compliment one another, to fit together to produce more activity. And, because the subdivision of labour can be made ever finer, there is a mutually reinforcing relationship between specialisation and greater efficiency, which feeds back into the growth of the market economy. For Smith the resulting differentiation of tasks gives rise to profitability of trade. Yet, for all his tributes to the benefits of specialisation he warned that in the progress of the division of labour, employment comes to be confined to a few simple operations. The consequence of the fragmentation of tasks is thus a simplification of competency to skill and skill to the successful completion of task. "The man whose whole life is spent in performing a few simple operations" he writes, "has no occasion to exert his understanding…He…generally becomes as stupid and ignorant as it is possible for a human creature to become."[7] In this paper I wish to explore how the educational process has been transformed into a mass product, how quality has been quantified, to see whether this transformation has altered educational content by converting critical reason into instrumental reason, imagination into passive pedantry, practical-virtue into skills accumulation and credit transfer; in effect learning into mental dryrot.[8]

### 1. Changes in Form and Effects on Content

A university can only exploit its global attractiveness if it has a recognisable product to circulate, indeed, only once a good or process is standardised can it be exchanged on the (soon to be) liberalised global market, and any market determines successful entry of a good according to its usefulness. In this global economy, where there is a particular distribution of labour intensive industries in cheaper production locations, advanced economies look to 'high-value' sectors to offset this transfer and, as previously stated, this means centring on high technology and increasingly biotechnology industries. One response to this has been to focus research funding on areas specifically useful to the performance of the nation's economy and another has been to equip a variety of workers for employment within these fields. In addition, because information is being generated at an alarming rate, the rather modern notion that professionals acquire a body of knowledge and then use this within their practice has been superseded by the idea that professionals require the skills to manipulate transient information.[9] In consequence, the need to devote curriculum time and emphasis to communicating knowledge and developing understanding has evaporated, "because today's knowledge goes rapidly out of date, and computers will supply what we need when we need it, in any case." [10] Instead of 'understanding,' allegedly higher level cognitive skills, such as 'reflection' and 'problem solving', and interpersonal abilities, for example 'communication skills', have become *the* valuable features of educational content and this has been drilled in to distinct disciplines through internal and external quality reviews.

One of the most insidious effects of quality enhancement is that the process of learning and teaching has been given a particular form or shape, which in effect has determined educational content. The process has been broken down into parts, each part quantified and measured against criteria largely imported from the Qualifications Framework and standardised benchmarked documents: the introduction of modularisation; transparent learning outcomes and assessment fitted to task. Each programme is expected to specify its content as outcomes, in terms of subject specific knowledge and specific skills, as well as more generic skills. The reduction of any margin for deviation and distortion between programmes at different institutions, effected by benchmarking, is a prerequisite for commercial delivery and the specification of content, in terms of skills-based outcomes, neatly manufactures a coincidence between programme and the expectations of a 'knowledge-economy.' Each programme is itself broken down into deliverable products or modules, which are assessed according to pre-specified weekly learning outcomes. The criteria, according to which a learner selects module and outcome, can only be ease of assessment and assimilation or folklore and preconception. At the same time, the fragmentation of modularisation encourages the student to select and abstract the part from the whole, simplify the object or ideas under consideration, and, in effect, to decontextualise both the object and the selection process. Hence we have learning situations where a student is presented with material and asked to offer Marxist, feminist, Leavisite and poststructuralist readings, as though each were a delectable item in an array of supermarket specials. The exchangeability of approach is indicative of an underlying commitment to the primacy of a singular skill: reflection.

In the situation where selection and abstraction seem to be desirable intellectual characteristics, the use of the term 'reflection' is a puzzle. In common parlance 'reflection' can mean one of three things. It can mean a physical reflection or the state of being reflected, such as by a mirror or a feedback loop from a video camera filming its own monitor. Reflection can also indicate an introspective awareness or being aware of one's subjective state. In addition, the term can indicate simply thinking hard about something. To consider something carefully, normally means to think about it according to the principles of reason. Philosophy, according to Max Horkheimer, once knew of no higher principle than reason,[11] as it was responsible for the origin of the Universe (*archē*), its organising principle (logos) and the categorical formation of the world. In these cases, reason can seem far removed from reflection, but the concept of reason, even in these instances, always includes the concept of critique; the willingness to bring into question the given, and indeed, what is not or cannot be given. Included in this, is a quest for the conditions of the principles of reason themselves. In such a case, reflection is the concern with what lies outside the regular, and mechanically reproducible, use of reasoning.

> If reflection were to be given a pattern of argument it might be something like this. Starting with common-sense realism, that there is a world 'out there' and that an account of that world is possible, reflection, then, considers the description of the world as elusive and perplexing because, somehow, no description adequately captures experience and knowledge of the world.[12]

Critique, however, always runs the risk of scepticism; the inability to find warrant for any foundation or justification for foundational principles. Critical reason, central to a life of practical-virtue, is thus transformed into instrumental reason. Reason, when stripped by scepticism of its affective content or ethical direction, tends to look for clear, perhaps simple, truths, so that it can methodically order them into an argument form in order to draw conclusions. The features of reason, in cases such as these, can then be summarised "as the optimum adaptation of means to ends…a pragmatic instrument oriented to expediency."[13] In summary, the tendencies to select, simplify and abstract, the very principles of reason presented to the student as hallmarks of appropriate learning, are the main features of instrumental reason: reason with neither ethical content nor sensitivity to context.14

Within the educational context, Schön, building on the Kolb cycle of reflection, suggests that the reflective practitioner is someone who reflects on his or her experience and generalises from this towards future action. Because the student considers his or her future learning needs by assessing prior learning difficulties, "it is a reflection which should lead to improved or at least carefully premeditated performance."[15] As the conditions of reflection are assumed and the principles purely absorbed, one could argue that the critical aspect of reflection has disappeared from view. The summary identification of needs and aspirations, alongside the judgment of successful or unsuccessful progress, seems to model effective learning on the principles of efficiency. In these cases, reasonable reflection adapts process to output, given the limits of the material, and contributes only the idea of systematic unity. By incorporating the criteria of successful performance, as the markers of appropriate reflective activity, reason must assume a faultless and harmonious cycle of educational production; thus turning a pre-conscious experience of work into an acceptable form of reflection or 'mindfulness.'

Without wishing to anthropomorphise reason, critical theorists are inclined to argue that when reason is disassociated from its affective content, criteria for reflection are likely to be identified with the needs of self-preservation. Hence it makes perfect sense for the learner to be as selective as the situation allows. To militate against this, the teacher is exhorted to create situations in which learners should not be able to escape without learning something. Grasping the reasonable nature of the students' principle of self-preservation, the lecturer also remembers that the 'something' used to be more than data processing. So, identifying the content of the course as 'effective reflection,' the lecturer is able to persuade him or herself, as well as the learner, that content assimilation is really in their objective interest and so feels morally justified in introducing continual formative and summative assessment. Thinking then becomes subjected to the discipline of testing, so that learning becomes the mere acquisition and reproduction of ideas, and each object of learning is a hurdle on the way to somewhere else. In such a passive-aggressive context, thought, perverted into the solving of assigned problems, processes everything it encounters as an exercise. The omnipresence of problem-based learning is testimony to the incorporation of critical reason into the surrounding apparatus. Because there is pay-off with successful performance, private thought finds itself in harmony with public interest, and reflection dissolves into more of the same.

Rather than prising students away from selection criteria, modelled on the social principle of performance, we have embedded and naturalised them within the academy. Because a quality learning experience requires the transmission of transferable skills, principally those that facilitate self-reflective learning, we are urged to introduce suitable assessments. This raises fundamental questions concerning not only appropriate forms of assessment but also the criteria used to determine whether the self is adequately reflective.[16] Indeed, how might the thinker reflect on him or her self and their learning process? The reflective student would approach the self as an object to be known, just as s/he has been shown to apprehend all objects of thought: material from which to generalise about problems and their solutions to guarantee future performance. The process seems premised on simplification and abstraction and the power of thought appears to be perverted into a vehicle for delivering success at the stipulated task. All this coincides neatly with the student's fine sense of instrumental self-preservation. Theodor Adorno, commenting on similar cultural processes, notes how generations reverse, the youth seeking its validation in the principle of reality, whilst the older generation digresses into the intelligible world, or, in today's clime, wanders into early retirement. The other option occasionally adopted is to become one with the tough necessity of the market: sharp suits and lap tops.

## 2. Changes in Delivery and Effects on Content

If educational content has been transformed through mutation of its form, adjustments to the manner of delivery have been, only marginally, less significant. As noted earlier, one consequence of the standardisation of the product is that it is, in principle, available to a plurality of already presupposed recipients. In the same way, the pre-digested quality of the educational product justifies and establishes itself all the more firmly in so far as it constantly refers to those who cannot digest anything not already masticated. Lecture notes and extracts on the web, essay plans and solutions to problems on e-mail, continual availability of the principle resource – the lecturer – all lend themselves to the belief that no student should encounter any difficulty when thinking through a problem. Students now expect to be given, or mailed, handouts with an itemised commentary that they can reproduce; indeed we are grateful when they are so reproduced. In the end, criticisms and solutions will be made available and handed out in party bags.

Just as a child's attention is difficult to keep for any length of time, every probationer is taught that a student must be presumed to have a limited attention span; everything must be spelt out. Each lecture is made up of familiar and easily recognisable and (through frequent repetition) generally accepted formulae, within an overall scheme that remains basically the same. Each lecture course presents itself in endlessly repeated generic module descriptors, listing week-by-week content and each is supposed to begin with three main bullet points, a segmented beginning, middle and end, and a final summary of content according to the initial points. A low level performance might use an Overhead Projector (OHP), but it is much better to Power Point these parcels of information, include a few animations, cartoons, pictures from the web and slogans zooming in from left to right. The students gaze at the screen, not even having to take notes because these are placed on their laps. This candyfloss and popcorn approach to lecturing communicates ideas as though each must excite, entertain and, most importantly, be fun. Wrestling from the process the proper expectation that learning is bound to be difficult, even, maybe especially, when it excites the imagination, we prejudge the material and encode the images and sound bites, reflecting back a muted but jazzed-up excitement, which is nothing at all. Such pleasure usually hardens into boredom because "if it is to remain pleasure, it must not demand any effort and therefore moves rigorously in the worn grooves of association."[17] Because no intellectual work must be expected from the learner, the development of an argument is presented in obviously incremental steps, each foothold selected due to its ease. All thought which is serious is considered a fault of the old fashioned and humourless - those academics who think of nothing but their own research.

One can draw a parallel with Adorno's remarks on mass culture. Commenting on American cinema, Adorno noted that it was no coincidence that cynical American film producers were heard to say that pictures must take into consideration the sophistication level of eleven year olds.[18] Adorno believed that, in fact, film moguls would like to make adults into eleven year olds. The supposition that we actually infantilise the learner is confirmed by the fact that sessions are supposed to begin with registration, absentees chased endlessly by notes and memos that can be reproduced as part of the audit trail: making a mockery of the idea of freely electing learners. Indeed feedback loops engineer the most childlike and unreflective commentary: 'how much did you enjoy your lecture?.' Where twice as many columns, in course evaluation documentation, are devoted to the lecturer's style and communication skills than to content, it could be said that form has triumphed over content, but, more significantly, is the fact that the learner is used to judge the lecturer as a more or less successful provider of learning.[19] In the *Wealth of Nations*, Adam Smith lamented the fact that the teacher's income was divorced from effectiveness. He thought it was a shame that the system, by presenting the teacher with a captive audience, excluded the exercise of consumer sovereignty. He would welcome the new educational context, where pay is to be determined in part by performance. Yet in this context, the feedback mechanism, for determining pay, is merely a conduit for judgments about excellence, nothing but the reproduction of existing forms of address, which all seems to come down to whether the lecturer can guarantee success and tell a few jokes along the way.

## 3. Technological Forces for Change

Reflective practitioners are required to consider their familiarity with information and communication technology, and competence in the new media is one principal desirable outcome of the learning experience; thus self-interest and general welfare are harmonised. New technology in the educational environment has become a force of production itself, altering a number of aspects of teaching and learning. Rather than the academic team directing the effects of this technology, there is a reduction of teaching, learning, and support work to simple elements within the global system. Embedding technological competence as a skill for both teacher and learner has altered the manner of delivery, and in its course altered the form, and so content, of the educational process, but also shifted the institutional organisation. New technology has accelerated and compelled the development of the market in higher education and it is worth examining how it has managed to compress the aims of education into the single aim of contributing to the performativity of the social system and the concomitant effect on labour itself.

Firstly, by detecting a parallel with modifications within the cultural sphere, it is possible to identify a few main modifications of teaching and learning. Mass education, as a subcategory of mass communication, institutes a fundamental break between the producer and recipient.[20] There is, in effect, an inverse proportional relationship between the splintering of the dialogic conditions of learning and 'quality assurance' references to the 'quality learning experience.' The recipient, although described variously as a customer or active participant, has little real input into course content and its packaging up into generic modular parcels. Although the flow of information is all one way there is an appearance of responsiveness, facilitated by new technologies. Each academic is expected to present information on the web; not only details of modules and reading lists but also selected web sites, connections to other on-line resources, early notification of essay questions and, undoubtedly, essay plans as well. Spammed daily by student requests for more, the lecturer attends to every demand as though it were a need, completing the infantilisation of the student. But the effect is to reduce conversation to an occasional problem-solving meeting between recipient and newly estranged producer. Even in these conversations, the relation to knowledge is not articulated in terms of the realisation of the life of the spirit but in terms of users of complex conceptual and material machinery. Thompson describes this type of relationship as 'mediated quasi-interaction' because, although there is an interaction, the flow of information is predominantly one way and the modes of response available to recipients are strictly circumscribed. Although the asymmetry of the communicative act does not affect complete passivity in the recipient, it does ensure that the conditions for interaction mute any careful reflection. Brainstorming about problems, as Lyotard notes, will become the generic template for seminars or tutorials. Fitted to its task, the appropriate method of assessment for this technology is multiple-choice. Reflecting the arduous cognitive demands of mass media, the student will inevitably be asked merely to answer whether Hume was an empiricist, an ecologist or Wednesday.

Secondly, communication technology, by separating social interaction from locale, also enables individuals to act for distant others. The potential for increased visibility affords both economic opportunity and risk and technical changes to internal delivery parallel the assessment that there is a global demand for educational services that support dynamic 'knowledge-based' economies.[21] Positioning the higher education sector of the United Kingdom as the fulcrum of provision, due to the high reputation of education institutions and the prominence of English language, the government has supported a number of projects designed to deliver distance e-based learning. And the development of distance learning, through technology enhanced by media such as the internet or satellite digital television, offers the possibility of cross-border supply of the educational product. By offering a way to retrain and reskill the labour force, technology driven distance learning is one way to guarantee the flexibility of education, ensuring its responsiveness to the needs of the business 'community.' Indeed, the very speed of technological development suggests a number of ways in which this global educational market will be structured, to avoid risk and exploit economic opportunity by concentrating on this ability to deliver the product across borders. Strategic alliances between higher educational institutions may rationalise and centralise educational delivery, to prevent repetition of lecture content. As brand image becomes the way to attract customers, there might be pressure to source teaching provision from a small group of high profile individuals within the alliance through flexible electronic delivery. Web-based platforms can even now offer interactive audio lectures, accompanied by video streaming, scrolling lecture text and on-line links to other documentation. Face to face contact could then be maintained with individual institutions offering a 'branch office service' in support of the global brand.[22]

Lastly, technology-enabled rationalisation will consequently have a significant impact on the organisation of production and this will reverberate throughout the academic team. In the same way as the expression industry is not to be taken literally when discussing the culture industry, likewise the term in education means standardisation and rationalisation of distribution techniques, rather than the process itself.[23] Through centralisation of core delivery, there could be an almost immediate reduction of the number of 'lecturer hours' required. Off the peg, one-size fits all, 'specially designed for the individual recipient,' modules will be accessed by all those who are either cross-border, or too busy with real concerns to sit through lectures or seminars. And to the extent that learning is translatable into computer language, technicians and career development officers could replace the traditional lecturer, who would find their role redescribed. Already out on a limb, truly replaceable academics will find that their own activities appear to be not only insignificant, but also irrational; as useless as armchair thinking. Those with an eye to self-preservation will attempt to demonstrate their productive efficiency, by attracting funding. Carving a niche, protecting but ultimately betraying their imaginative spontaneity, academics are already so heavily committed to what is endorsed in their isolated sphere, so at odds with endless extolling of virtues of interdisciplinarity, that we no longer desire that which is not authenticated through the arduous process of peer review endorsement. Ambition aims solely at expertise in the accepted stock-in-trade, hitting on the correct slogan, the correct way to write a grant or book proposal, where claims of originality are evidenced through deliverable outcomes, set against those already on the market. In sway to this production process, the purpose of reason dwindles until it sinks into the fetishism of itself and stoically rests at ease with the necessity of the status quo.

## 4. From Process to Product

The combined effect of quality assurance regimes and mechanisms to distribute funding has been to deliver the second two performance objectives: reskilling and retraining the workforce and, alongside the benefits accrued from technological advancement, global 'competitiveness.' As noted, the commercialisation of the higher education sector requires there to be an exchangeable product, which can be delivered to multiple recipients and so far I have concentrated on how a process has been transformed into such a product. But, the peculiarity of the system is that the product is actually that which is the difference between the student, who is also the customer, on entry and student on exit. This 'value-added' quality is evidenced in the degree result, the transformation of thinking according to the model of instrumental efficiency, and the ability to package useful skills (Portfolios of Development). Because the recipient is a customer, the product needs to be successfully delivered, however, it is not the teaching that has to be delivered but the learning. This apparent contradiction is actually ironed out by the Quality Assurance Agency (QAA), which judges learning 'failures' and poor retention rates to be characteristics of a failing department, and consequently penalises the institution financially. Each student (has a right to) expect a 2:1, and soon every student shall receive one.

Commercialisation would be meaningless without a product with an exchange-value and it is this that provides the rationale for the introduction of job evaluation schemes. Job evaluation schemes will make it coherent to consider the average amount of labour required to perform newly specified tasks and so to manufacture a figure based on the socially necessary labour time required to deliver the product. That said, it is still the case that there are only limited ways a market-oriented educational sector can generate profit. First, and most obviously, income will be derived from the differential margin between what staff can produce and what staff are paid; a numbers game. Secondly, because the time we can work is, contrary to indicators, inelastic, there is the option to reduce the salary bill. Liberalisation of the education market will probably lead to an increased number of academics from areas where academic labour is cheaper and thus there will be a continual momentum downwards; a momentum exacerbated by the drift towards local or individual pay bargaining. Finally, and most interestingly, given the recent heated debates concerning graduated top-up fees, extra income for institutions could be secured if price were to deviate from value. When universities charge graduated fees, the evidence for the apparent worth of the product will be the ratio that the outputs, degree awards, stand to one another in the competitive market. A ratio already prejudged by the graduated fee and supported by the social mechanism.

Pressure to liberalise the education market, to remove legal, regulatory and bureaucratic barriers distorting 'market competition' has followed from the commercialisation of the sector. But while liberalisation, at the level of the General Agreement on Trade in Services (GATS), is a response to the commercialisation of the sector, there is an internal dynamic as well. Alongside the casualisation of staffing contracts, is a tendency to reorientate research funding towards short-term, competitive project grants, the allocation of which can be rather prescriptive, and a tendency to manage the 'business' of education. The effect of competitive funding and performance measurement has been an exponential increase in the administrative burden, in the form of grants applications and time management submissions, as well as the emergence of a new oligarchic form of robust management. Commercialisation of the sector has required the management of a shift from academic liberal, tenured, sensitivity to a sensibility that can accept the highly intrusive and prescriptive quality regime and the most casualised working conditions outside the fast-food industry. The management, which has been peculiarly effective, has occurred through the quality assurance process itself.

Ashby once suggested that the beauty of the British collegiate system of university management was that it eliminated the administration as a power point. Retrospectively we can see that once this bureaucracy was professionalised there could be and was an imperceptible substitution of collegial, if even then rather oligarchic, form of self-management for a more hardy form of self-regulation. In universities today, management involves making educational provision and social organisation compatible with the demands of international economic system and it is doubtful that the aims of the educational sector could have been pulled into line without parallel commercialisation. I have already suggested that the combined effect of quality assurance pedagogical imperatives, alongside directed funding allocations, manufactured a product from a process. It is also the case that the same processes facilitate compliant individual and group responses to the auditing packages. Morley explains that because quality assurance is a socially constructed domain of power, with its own discourse that yields the power to inform and regulate, members of the academic team have had to incorporate and internalise it for their professional and organisational survival.

> The ruler no longer says: 'You must think as I do or die'. He says: 'You are free not to think as I do; your life, your property, everything shall remain yours, but from this day on you are a stranger among us'. Not to conform means to be rendered powerless...When the outsider is excluded from concern, he can only too easily be accused of incompetence. [24]

The cultural logic of quality inserts cognitive authority and elicits emotional power. Silencing all that might be critical, the language of quality suppresses any disturbance on the calm waters of managerial unanimity by indicating that non-compliance would render the individual untrustworthy, incompetent or morally repugnant. There is something insidious about the language of continuous improvement that fits well with the worthy, yet misplaced, sense of guilt felt by those who do not have to suffer the bustle of commerce and are glad of it.

For some of those who are administered, quality administration is an external affair, by which they are subsumed rather than comprehended, and where extrinsic norms, with nothing to do with the quality of the object, are imposed as abstract standards. Others, pretend to concede, without realising that there is no pretence, that 'objective quality' means the noncontroversial aspect of things, the unquestioned impression, the façade made up of classified data. Common sense encourages us to be cynical - or ironic - and to narrow down our aims in order to apply the most efficient means to them and evidence their attainment. However, common sense is often misleading and any 'quality-proofed' institution can provide a standardised good, be it a firm involved in a strategic partnership with a university, or Microsoft and Motorola and our continual repetition of pedagogical mantras, mimicking the voices of personnel officers, merely induces the same intellectual sluggishness we instil in others. That we can convince ourselves it is better to do it to ourselves before others do it to us, must indicate our own instillation into the general system, yet it is also the case that if it did have to be done then somehow doing it to ourselves seems to preserve our autonomy. It is false, though, in that we know how to do it all the more finely and rigorously, and the much-referenced necessity is only the market semblance of natural law. This final congruence of internal and external quality review brings the individual into line; estranged from product, production process, other members of the academic team, and from their own critical reason. What began as an ironic gesture has since submitted to the competitive reality of the possessive individualism of academic life.

Lyotard described how principles of performativity provoke a legitimation crisis in knowledge and defined the moment as post-modern. It seems to me on reflection that the standardisation of the product marks the moment as thoroughly modern. One effective difference is that the old language of administration took note of the relative autonomy of distinct spheres, for example distinctions between culture or education and administration, whereas the new administration unites all that is heteronomous, so absorbing all that might be critical. It is no accident that the jargon of authenticity (self-directed learning, widening participation, social inclusion, empowerment, motivated citizens) is spoken everywhere, at the point when the features of abstraction, selection, simplification and scepticism mark thought as instrumental. In this sense Adam Smith was right. The self-regulating mechanism is primarily a means of achieving widening markets, promoting growth, developing the division of labour. But no market is ever free and the political pressure of quality and funding regimes weave together finely tuned directives, restructuring higher education to accommodate the functional needs of an old industrial power within a global economy. Because efficiency, due to the division of labour, does have its price, perhaps we are, as Smith remarked, as stupid and ignorant as it is possible for human creatures to become, and so, because the functional ends are hidden from view, we allow the false appearance of harmony to speak in the name of social justice.

## Notes

[1] Amelie Rorty, *Philosophers on Education: New Historical Perspectives* (London: Routledge, 1998), 1-11.
[2] Alfred Whitehead, *The Aims of Education and Other Essays* (London: Ernest Benn Limited, 1962), 139.
[3] Ibid, 4.
[4] Gillian Howie and Ashley Tauchert, *Gender, Teaching and Research: Challenges for the 21$^{st}$ Century* (Hampshire: Ashgate, 2002).

This current paper develops an argument begun in Gillian Howie, 'A Reflection of Quality: Instrumental Reason, Quality Audits and the Knowledge Economy' in *Critical Quarterly*, 2002.

[5] Jean-Francis Lyotard, *The Postmodern Condition: A Report of Knowledge* (Manchester: Manchester University Press, 1986), 53.

[6] Joseph Cropsey, *Polity and Economy: an interpretation of the principles of Adam Smith* (The Hague, Nijhoff 1957) 165-76.

[7] Adam Smith, *The Essential Adam* Smith, ed. Robert. Heilbroner, (Oxford: Oxford University Press 1986), 302.

[8] Whitehead, 2.

[9] Louise Morley, *Quality and Power in Higher Education* (Maidenhead: Open University Press, 2003), 7.

[10] John Cowan, *On Becoming an Innovative University Teacher: Reflection and Action* (Maidenhead: Open University Press, 1998), 29.

[11] Max Horkheimer, The End of Reason in ed Andrew Arato and Eike Gebhart., *The Essential Frankfurt School Reader* (Oxford: Basil Blackwell,1978) 26-48

[12] Julian Roberts, *The Logic of Reflection: German Philosophy in the Twentieth Century* (New Haven and London: Yale University Press, 1992), 5-11, 281-286.

[13] Horkheimer, *op cit.*, 28.

[14] For a discussion of instrumental reason see Jay Bernstein, *Adorno: Disenchantment and Ethics* (Cambridge: Cambridge University Press 2001) 76, 89-98, 137-9.

[15] Cowan, 36.

[16] David Baume and Mantz Yorke, "The Reliability of Assessment by Portfolio in a Course to Develop and Accredit Teachers in Higher Education," *Studies in Higher Education* 27 (2002): 8-25.

[17] Theodor Adorno and Max Horkheimer, *The Dialectic of the Enlightenment*, trans. John Cumming (London: Verso, 1986), 137.

[18] Theodor Adorno, *The Culture Industry: Selected Essays on Mass Culture*, ed. Jay Bernstein (London: Routledge, 1991), 91.

[19] Morley, 130.

[20] For a discussion of mass media and technology see John Thompson, *Ideology and Modern Culture: Critical Social Theory in the Era of Mass* Culture, (Cambridge: Polity Press, 1990).

[21] Merrill Lynch estimated this demand to be in excess of US $2 trillion per year, figure quoted Alex Nunn, The General Agreement on Trade in Services: An Impact Assessment for Higher Education in the UK, AUT 2001, 10.

[22] *Ibid*, 14.

[23] Adorno, 87.

[24] Adorno and Horkheimer, 133.

# Bibliography

Adorno, Theodor. *The Culture Industry: Selected Essays on Mass Culture* ed., Jay Bernstein. London: Routledge, 1991.

Adorno, Theodor and Max Horkheimer. *The Dialectic of the Enlightenment*. Trans. John Cumming. 2$^{nd}$ ed. London: Verso, 1986.

Arato, Andrew and Eike Gebhardt. *The Essential Frankfurt School Reader*. Oxford: Basil Blackwell, 1978.

Baume, David and Mantz Yorke. "The Reliability of Assessment by Portfolio in a Course to Develop and Accredit Teachers in Higher Education" *Studies in Higher Education* vol 27, no 1 (2002) 8-25.

Bernstein, Jay. *Adorno: Disenchantment and Ethics*. Cambridge: Cambridge University Press, 2001.

Cowan, John. *On Becoming an Innovative University Teacher: Reflection and Action*. Maidenhead: Open University Press, 1998.

Cropsey, Joseph. *Polity and Economy: An Interpretation of the Principles of Adam Smith*. The Hague: Nojhoff, 1957.

Horkheimer, Max. The End of Reason in *The Essential Frankfurt School Reader*, eds., Andrew Arato and Eike Gebhardt Oxford: Basil Blackwell, 1978

Howie, Gillian. "A Reflection of Quality: Instrumental Reason, Quality Audits and the Knowledge Economy" in *Critical Quarterly* 44:4 (2002).

Howie, Gillian and Tauchert, Ashley, *Gender, Teaching and Research*. Hampshire: Ashgate 2002.

Lyotard, Jean-Francis. *The Postmodern Condition: A Report of Knowledge*. 1$^{st}$ pub as La Condition postmoderne: rapport sur le savoir by Les Editions de Minuit (1979). Manchester: Manchester University Press, 1986.

Morley, Louise. *Quality and Power in Higher Education*. Maidenhead: Open University Press, 2003.

Nunn, Alex. The General Agreement on Trade in Services: An Impact Assessment for Higher Education in the UK. Association of University Teachers, 2001.

O'Driscoll, Gerald. Adam *Smith and the Modern Political Economy*. Iowa: Iowa State University Press, 1979.

Roberts, Julian. *The Logic of Reflection: German Philosophy in the Twentieth Century*. New Haven and London: Yale University Press, 1992.

Rorty, Amelie. *Philosophers on Education: New Historical Perspectives*. London: Routledge, 1998.

Smith, Adam. *The Essential Adam Smith*. Edited by Robert. Heilbroner. Oxford: Oxford University Press, 1986.

Thompson, John. *Ideology and Modern Culture: Critical Social Theory in the Era of Mass Culture*. Cambridge: Polity Press, 1990.

West, Edwin. *Adam Smith: The Man and his Works*. Indianapolis: Liberty Fund, 1976.

Whitehead, Alfred. *The Aims of Education and Other Essays*. London: Ernest Benn Limited, 1962.

# CHAPTER THREE

## Emergent Skills in Higher Education: The Quest for Emotion and Virtual University

*Luis Borges Gouveia*

**Abstract:**
Over the past twenty years various new models and strategies of Information and Communication Technologies (I.C.T.) have been developed. Many of these view time and space constraints in a different way. Additionally the information and knowledge society requires new skills to both the professional and the learner. Within considering a higher education context, the need to deal with change, innovation and evolving models of competition and collaboration brings new challenges.

Although higher education deals traditionally in sharing ideas, experimentation and reflection, it is not as good at listening to these ideas. Presental teaching, organisational structures, administrative processes, curricula organisation and knowledge sharing strategies are much more onerous tasks because many higher education newcomers are unwilling to learn the skills that the so-called information and knowledge society demands of them.

The use of virtuality, considered here as the desmaterialisation of learning settings and experiences, provides the opportunity to cope with time and space constraints and to innovate both on practices and on what individuals need to know. This chapter discusses the skills that may emerge from adopting a virtual approach to higher education and its likely impact.

Keywords: Space and Time; Higher Education; Virtual Learning; Information Society.

## 1. Introduction

Some years ago, I perceived the University as the house of knowledge. It seemed that the best ideas and deep theories generally came from inside its walls. It is at the University that people discuss and shape both the science and technology that could change society. It thus plays a central strategic position and turns the University as a central player even when political concerns are at stake.

People within the University, particularly its professors, have the responsibility as gatekeepers of knowledge and provide the last word on available truth. They have the ability to compile available information, process it, and more importantly put it into perspective with more classic views. Finally they can provide insight into what others could do with available knowledge.

The interesting point is that, as a result of the University's success in both providing knowledge to society and training people in its use, the university role itself has changed dramatically. The University is no longer the definitive place where knowledge lives and is put forward.

A number of evolving phenomena concerning the way knowledge is generated, processed and delivered needs to be addressed by the University. The University is challenged by other players such as the media, government and not for profit institutions concerning its role as a knowledge builder and gatekeeper. Among those phenomena, a number of issues are of interest for this discussion.

## 2. The Case of Information Society

The 'information society' is a term used to describe a society and an economy that makes the best possible use of I.C.T. The information society can be seen as providing the means of creating, distributing, and manipulating knowledge. As a result, the information society has become the most significant driver for economic and cultural activity.

In such a society individuals can expect to take advantage of the full benefits that technology can provide at work and at home. The use of commodities such as internet banking services, Automatic Teller Machines, mobile phones, teletext television, internet e-mail and the World Wide Web, provide examples of the impact of I.C.T. on modern society.

These new technologies have implications for all aspects of our society and economy; they are changing the way in which we do business, how we learn and how we spend our leisure time. They also provide new challenges to governments:

1) Create appropriate laws to support the new social, business and leisure activities created by the information society;
2) To educate all in the use of technology-based services and applications;
3) Ensure the smooth passage to electronic-based businesses, in order to assure their competitiveness;
4) Develop more modern local and central government systems using the technology to empower the public in taking benefit of the knowledge and services available

IBM proposes a definition for the information society as,

> a society characterised by a high level of information intensity in the everyday life of most citizens, in most organisations and workplaces; by the use of common or

compatible technology for a wide range of personal, social, educational and business activities, and by the ability to transmit, receive and exchange digital data rapidly between places irrespective of distance.[1]

For some authors information society seems to be the way of either describing technologically driven tendencies and opportunities of our societies, or legitimising certain public policies such as those produced by the European Commission as presented on the e-Europe action plan.[2]

Overall, we can view the information society as an overworked expression that has been used to denote many different concepts. The sense in which it is most commonly used refers to a growing high-technology based, materially affluent service society where information rather than raw materials or energy is the dominant technology.[3] Some would argue that it strives toward a society characterised by increasing responsiveness towards individual human needs, and toward preserving ecological balances.

Since society has always been dependent on information, one can argue that we have always been an information society. That is, there has always been a rudimentary information infrastructure. For thousands of years society's dependence on information was not apparent as the quality of information was small enough that it could be remembered and passed on in an oral tradition.[4] Today, a number of issues such as complexity, quality, quantity and time create conditions that require the use of I.C.T. in conjunction with the use of a digitally based information.

Isabel Álvarez and Brent Kilbourn propose an overview of information society literature[5]. This shows different authors conceptualising the character of the information society in different ways; some emphasising different topics and treating those topics from varying perspectives. They also argue that a considerable portion of the literature is devoted to discussions about how we must move from our present reductionist, mechanistic ways of seeing the world to more connected, holistic, inclusive ways of thinking.

## 3. Key Issues in the Current Status of Higher Education

Saying that education, learning and training is dynamic is neither a new concept or position. In fact, many authors from different generations report changes both in the way education can be delivered and on technologies used for such delivery. Despite this diverse discussion the higher education model has remained virtually the same since the introduction of universities hundred of years ago.

Recent times have raised issues and questions which the University needs to address in order to accomplish its role of higher education within society:

1) Increase use of I.C.T. and the drive towards the digital offers a different model for delivery education. Multimedia, the use of computers and communications and powerful applications such as World Wide Web and email are now widely used and together can provide a new learning environment.
2) Due to enhanced media and communications, information is much more visible now. Knowledge is thus attainable faster than ever, creating the potential problem with people having to cope with information overload.
3) Time and space constraints are now different and people can have a double presence: the physical one and a virtual one which provides new forms of contact and a variety of alternative styles and self-identification. This means that each individual now has new forms to identify himself and to perceive others.
4) The number of educated people is growing. This means that an increased number of people are now able to advance knowledge and provide critical insight concerning not only their activity but also the knowledge that will be used.
5) The nature of knowledge itself is more complex. It is much more integrated, with a wider range of disciplines and each day more difficult for a single individual to cope with.

Together, these issues demand a completely different approach to deal with the information needed for modern society. As a result, a new set of skills is now needed and this may be a real problem for universities concerning the way they organise their main activity of furthering knowledge (research) and higher education (training).

## 4. Individual Skills for the Information Society

A number of skills can be considered to better enable each individual to make use of the emergent opportunities in the information society. They must assure a minimum competence level and fulfil the following requirements:

1) *ability to perform*: know how to do and to act in new situations and contexts;
2) *work capacity*: demonstrate ability to work under pressure, both individually and in groups;
3) *flexibility*: each individual must be able to work under different contexts and to take decisions and cope with change;
4) *self learner*: be able to learn alone as well as within ones own needs;
5) *reporting*: be able to analyse a situation and to outline it. This will assure the individual role as a communicator;

6) *creative*: considering the need to be a leader, to propose new perspectives, to take winning decisions and be proactive.
7) *collaborate*: be able to work with other in such way they compound individual contributions with others' contributions in order to achieve a better result from the 'collective thinking.'
8) *share information*: be able to share information with others and provide a 'open position' to others.
9) *representing information*: be able to convey to others information both actively reducing its complexity and simplifying its structure. Additionally, representation is a key skill concerning issues such as in determining the quantity and quality of information.
10) *information proactive*: be able to select information sources, access information and search for answers. This means that the individual must perform the relevant questions and use the appropriate filters to construct the information.

Such skills form a long and ambitious list of desirables for an educated individual in our information society. They represent a number of skills that must be present to deal with the issues of information overload as well as to enforce individuals understanding.[6]

A number of authors present such a list as more high level skill and refer to it as critical thinking. In particular Michael Scriven and Richard Paul describe it as,

> the intellectually disciplined process of actively and skillfull conceptualising, applying, analysing, synthesising, and/or evaluating information gathered from, or generated by, observation, experience, reflection, reasoning, or communication, as a guide to belief and action.[7]

Critical thinking can be seen as having two components: a set of skills to process and generate information and beliefs, and the habit, based on intellectual commitment, of using those skills to guide behaviour. Critical thinking is not the acquisition and retention of information alone, or the possession of a set of skills, or even the mere use of specific skills without reflect over their results. Rather, critical thinking is usually a matter of degree, and is dependent upon, among other things, the quality and depth of experience in a given domain of thinking or with respect to a particular class of questions. The development of critical thinking skills is seen as a life-long endeavor[8].

This chapter suggests that the above list of skills is an essential path to develop within the individual the ability to deal with information and foster its critical thinking skills.

## 5. Four Levels of Literacy for the Information Society Individual

To be part of the information society four levels of literacy must be acquired. These levels describe the general skills that any individual must have in order to be able to take advantage of the opportunities provided. Some of these are quite basic and commonplace but others require new approaches to deal with.

The four levels of literacy are:

1) *basic literacy*: to read and write and to use the language. Nowadays, along with the native language, it is expected that at least another language can be used with a regular level of proficiency.
2) *technological literacy*: to use and take advantage of I.C.T, in particular the computer. Knowledge of the most common applications of word processing, spreadsheets, number crunching, presentation, and databases are needed. Additionally, some degree of skill in using computers to solve problems as needed.
3) *information literacy*: how to use information systematically and develop critical use of information. This level in particular is very important as it provides individuals with the tools to become more efficient in their use of information in their daily lives.
4) *communication literacy*: group interaction is extremely important. It provides the necessary skills related to human communication and leadership. This may include self-motivation and group motivation as well as reporting and negotiating skills.

These last two levels, information literacy and communication literacy, are major concerns in the information and communication society and provide an opportunity to foster education renewal.

A number of issues arise when we discuss the actions needed to assure each of these four kinds of literacy. Past experience concerning basic literacy, and more recently the efforts over technological literacy, can provide important insight on how difficult it can be to extend and improve existing literacy levels for all people. This chapter argues that the University has an important role in improving such literacy levels, in particular the information and communication literacy.

## 6. Emergent Skills in Higher Education

Maurice Duverger suggests the 21st Century will become known as 'the community's century,' as the 5th Century has been known as the city's century, and the 14th Century as the state's century.[9] Following the same author, the trend is towards the growth of the community both in number and quality, as well as the union of the states, without losing their identities.

The interaction between states establishes a mutual enrichment, based on information exchange of their history, their culture and language, and shared values. The sharing of knowledge fosters society's development, not only economic, but also social, cultural and even political. Higher education must provide the necessary skills to enhance knowledge sharing and foster the skills that provide a true global citizenship. Information literacy and communication literacy are major concerns for society and present an important issue to the development and planning of strategies for an information and knowledge society.

This chapter takes the following positions:

1) information literacy can be defined as the ability to recognise when information is needed and to know where we can find it, and how to assess and use information in an effective way;[10]
2) important skills concerning information are the ability to access, use and understand various information sources. People are needed who possess information skills, and are able to perform information analysis, identify search strategies and obtain results;[11]
3) the individual must be able to understand and analyse what is being perceived, that is which information to sort, identify, select and analyse;[12]
4) a list of skills associated with the information and knowledge society:
   a. recognise that complete information is needed to better decision making;
   b. recognise the need of information;
   c. be able to draw questions based on its information needs;
   d. identify potential information sources;
   e. develop successful information search strategies;
   f. access information sources based on computer and other technologies;
   g. be able to assess information and information value;
   h. be able to organise information for its practical application;
   i. be able to integrate new information in a previous existent body of knowledge;
   j. be able to use information to critical thinking and to problem solving;[13]

As proposed by Manuel Castells, the network is an essential organisation model to connect people and to enhance individual power through its ability to deal with information.[14] This is opposed to the traditional isolation of those who have the knowledge. This chapter believes in a mooth but inevitable transformation towards the use of this network. This requires new knowledge and skills to be developed.

## 7. A Virtual University Approach: The Netlab Concept

University Fernando Pessoa, Portugal has set up as a freshman requirement, that every student must have a laptop computer. This requirement, started in 1995, makes the university a very rich computer environment. Today there is also a large number (70%) of university staff with computers too, covering the majority of the university academic areas.[15]

One of the most important goals of this project is to give to all students, from any major, a technological experience which will develop usefull computer skills. The idea behind this policy was to introduce laptops as the next multipurpose tool, and use them as a substitute for the traditional 'pen and paper' paradigm. New initiatives for continuing the current project include the use of Personal Access Devices (PADs), which function as a book, a notebook and a pen.

To offer more communication facilities between students, University Fernando Pessoa started a local area network with entry points in classrooms and other locations on campus. Also, the university offers free access to internet services and local university information system infrastructures such as administrative, pedagogic and library facilities. The use of internet/intranet act as a huge digital information resource for students' activities. Thus creating a learning environment rich in technology. This environment including the presence of laptops, network entry points in multiple campus locations, and Internet facilities, is termed, by the author as NetLab.

Within the NetLab, every student can connect to the network infrastructure using its own laptop through the campus facilities. Students are able to use networked facilities, and set up projects on their area. The uniform use of laptop computers is now part of the IT infrastructure of the university. This affects the use of a Campus Wide Information System.[16]

It is possible to consider the technological infrastructure just as the first layer that enables the production, communication, change and sharing of content among the various users on campus.

The second layer is content (quantity and quality), which is a very important factor. Higher education institutions are the great producers of content material and have a proper workforce to maintain these materials. To get the students involvement and even other teachers' involvement, it is necessary to gather content and publish it online.[17]

At the third layer, stands the NetLab. The NetLab intends to be neither a virtual campus network nor a distance learning environment. It wants to be a local interaction engine that provides a structured approach to services and content generated both by students and professors. But what is really different in NetLab?

First, it is people-centered rather than technology oriented. Second, the environment where NetLab exists has a strong reinforcement in mobility (with laptops and DHCP network entry points). Third, it provides a greater involvement between students and the university through the sharing of technology investments. Finally, because the network allows the use of tools for information manipulation from anywhere on campus, the NetLab can be seen as a first step to prepare and prototype on-line material and off-campus on-line courses.

When integrating these goals with the various resources, the institution can shift to offer on-line degrees off-campus and offering Open and Distance Learning (ODL) courses as a normal part of its service catalogue which define the last layer: the 'virtual university.' This situation has been defined as corresponding to the ones in reporting as virtual university.[18,19]

Figure 1 helps illustrate the role of NetLab as an educational lab that introduces innovative practices and that takes advantage of the Fernando Pessoa University environment.

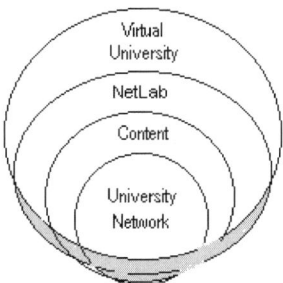

**Figure 1: The NetLab concept**

## 8. Final remarks

It seems that a lot remains to be done. This defines by itself the huge challenge that university and higher education must do to provide answers: its own change towards a more oriented skill approach where people become central.

One of the main challenges is to abandon the knowledge-centric approach. The University is not the restricted physical space where knowledge resides anymore. The University must take into account that the 'game' is not with data and information, but with information and knowledge and thus requires a new kind of university. This means that it is even more important to provide critical skills on where, who, what, when and why to use information and knowledge. As a result, a number of questions must be posed. For example, are knowledge-oriented degrees for a given area (sociology, computer science) still is the best approach? As a final point, we must remember that it is people who need information and thus, the motivation for learning is bound to emotion. One of the keywords to be regarded when we want to bind technology, information and people. This is also true for higher education.

## Notes

[1] IBM, "The Net Result - Report of the National Working Party for Social Inclusion," *IBM Community Development Foundation Report* (Houston, USA: IBM, 1997).

[2] European Commission, "The e-Europe 2002 Action Plan" Launched at the European Council in Feira, Portugal. June, 2000.

[3] IGNOU, "What is Information Society?" *A Primer or Information* Society (India: Indira Gandhi National Open University, 1998).

[4] Ibid.

[5] Isabel Álvarez and Brent Kilbourn, "Mapping the Information Society Literature: Topics, Perspectives, and Root Metaphors," *First Monday*, volume 7, number 1 (January 2002)

[6] Richard Saul Wurman, et al *Information Anxiety 2*. [book on line] (Chicago, Illinois: Que Press, 14 December 2000, accessed 21 March 2002); available from Que, www.quepublishing.com.

[7] Michael Scriven and Richard Paul, "Defining Critical Thinking," A draft statement for the National Council for Excellence in Critical Thinking (21 April 2003). <http://www.criticalthinking.org/University/univclass/Defining.html>

[8] Ibid.

[9] Maurice Duverger, *Droit, institutions et systèmes politiques*. Mélanges en hommage à Maurice Duverger. Paris: Presses universitaires de France, 1987.

[10] Robert Burnhein, "Information literacy - a core competency," *Australian Academic and Research Libraries*. 23:4 (1992):188-96.

[11] Mary Lenox and Michael Walker, "Information literacy in the educational process," *The Educational Forum*. 57:2 (1993):312-324.

[12] Mary Lenox and Micahel Walker, Information literacy: challenge for the future. *International Journal of Information and Library Research.* 4:1 (1992):1-18.
[13] Christina Doyle "Information Literacy in an Information Society: A Concept for the Information Age" adapted from ERIC monograph 23 August 2003,
< http://www.libraryinstruction.com/information-literacy2.html >
[14] Manuel Castells, *The Internet Galaxy* (Oxford: Oxford University Press, 2002).
[15] Luis Borges Gouveia, "The NetLab experience. Moving the action to electronic learning environments," In proceedings of BITE international conference. Maastricht, The Netherlands: 25-27 March, 1998: 395-405.
[16] Luis Borges Gouveia, "Group assessment: alternative forms to evaluate student skills," *Revista da UFP*, no. 2, vol. 2, (May 1998): 519-526.
[17] Ibid.
[18] Jon Mason, *Communities, networks, and education* (Melbourne: Ph.D. thesis University of Melbourne, 1999).
[19] Parker Rossman, Parker, *Information age – global higher education* (New York: Praeger: 1993).

## Bibliography

Álvarez, Isabel and Kilbourn. Brent "Mapping the Information Society Literature: Topics, Perspectives, and Root Metaphors." *First Monday*, volume 7, number 1 (January 2002).

Burnhein, Robert. Information literacy – a core competency. *Australian Academic and Research Libraries.* 23:4 (1992):188-96.

Castells, Manuel. *The Internet Galaxy*. Oxford: Oxford University Press, 2002.

Doyle, Christina "Information Literacy in an Information Society: A Concept for the Information Age" adapted from ERIC monograph 23 August 2003.
< http://www.libraryinstruction.com/information-literacy2.html >

Duverger, Maurice. *Droit, institutions et systèmes politiques*. Mélanges en hommage à Maurice Duverger. Paris: Presses universitaires de France, 1987.

European Commission. "The e-Europe 2002 Action Plan." Launched at the European Council in Feira, Portugal: June, 2000.

Gouveia, Luis Borges. "The NetLab experience. Moving the action to electronic learning environments." In proceedings of BITE international conference, Maastricht, The Netherlands, 25-27 March 1998, pp. 395-405.

Gouveia, Luis Borges. "Group assessment: alternative forms to evaluate student skills." *Revista da UFP*, no 2, vol. 2, May (1998): 519-526.

IBM. "The Net Result - Report of the National Working Party for Social Inclusion," *IBM Community Development Foundation Report*. Houston, USA: 1997.

IGNOU. "What is Information Society?" *A Primer on Information Society*. India: Indira Gandhi National Open University, 1998.

Lenox, Mary and Walker Michael "Information literacy: challenge for the future." *International Journal of Information and Library Research.* 4:1 (1992):1-18.

Lenox, Mary and Walker, Michael. "Information literacy in the educational process." *The Educational Forum.* 57:2 (1993):312-324.

Mason, Jon *Communities, networks, and education* Ph.D. thesis (Melbourne: University of Melbourne, 1999).

Rossman, Parker. *Information age - global higher education.* New York Praeger, 1993.

Scriven, Michael and Richard Paul, "Defining Critical Thinking" A draft statement for the National Council for Excellence in Critical Thinking (21 April 2003) <http://www.criticalthinking.org/University/univclass/Defining.html>

Wurman, Richard, Loring Leifer and David Sume *Information Anxiety 2*. [book on line] Chicago, Illinois: Que Press, 14 December 2000, accessed 21 March 2002. www.quepublishing.com

# CHAPTER FOUR

# Myths and Realities of Higher Education as a Vehicle for Nation Building in Developing Countries: The Culture of the University and the New African Diaspora

## Seth A. Agbo

**Abstract**
One of the challenges facing Africa as it enters the twenty-first century is the dilemma created by lack of economic growth. Since the 1960s the main views of the advancement of Africa have been characterised by the dominance of three concurrent and paradoxical development theories: 1) the modernisation theory; 2) the human capital theory; and, 3) the dependency theory. All three of these theories owe a good measure of their effect and pervasiveness to the impact of the university. These theories also reflect the contradictions of the lopsided processes of socio-economic development that have been extended from the centres of higher learning in Western Europe and North America since the advent of the university to its peripheries in Africa, Asia, and Latin America. The thesis of this chapter is that the processes of higher education have not always resulted in development. The African university, like its counterpart in the advanced developed world, has maintained a stubborn resistance to change as it strives to remain protected from external interference from the local community. The immediate consequence of this is that the artificial environment of the African university helps only to serve the interests of the former colonial powers.

Key Words: developing countries; modernisation theory; human capital theory; dependency theory; socio-economic development; higher education policy; university culture; brain drain; colonialism; African diaspora.

## 1. Introduction

When colonies in the Third World started clamouring for political independence, politicians of the West demonstrated to the world that newly independent countries could sustain development if they adopted Western strategies. Two of the strategies, the *human capital* and *modernisation* theories became so attractive that since independence in the late 1950s and 1960s, developing nations have placed much emphasis on education as a vehicle for modernisation and socio-economic development. The movement to expand educational opportunities in Africa was strongly tied to economic development and technocratic visions of societal reconstruction. Changes in political and economic environments do not deter governments from continuing to invest in higher education. There is a belief that such an investment will generate direct benefits to the state in by providing the necessary high-level manpower and carrying out development-oriented research. Investment in higher education would also in many ways serve the needs of society by rendering various services and advice to policy-makers.

Because the movement to expand educational opportunities in the developing world was strongly tied to socio-economic development, higher education has remained an area in which most developing countries maintain a strong commitment although it continues to fail to produce the desired results. In Africa, industrialisation, modernisation, secularisation, economic growth, employment creation, import substitution, social engineering, manpower development, and so on, were the key slogans that dominated the higher education scheme that began after independence. African development was then conceived as an attempt to come up to the living standards of more industrialised countries by adopting development methods used in those countries.

Despite the many efforts made by various African governments to invest in higher education and to bridge the development gap between their countries and the advanced industrialised world, their investment remains unproductive to national development. The educational processes and the material costs of education are at the root of the contemporary crises of national development. In other words, while increasing expenditure on higher education to provide essential infrastructures for national development, higher education also threatens national development to an unprecedented degree. For example, the type of education bequeathed to Africa by colonialism has only succeeded in producing a new educated elite. From its inception, education has acted as ammunition in the hands of the educated elite to migrate to the developed countries. The new elite who, for the want of any better terminology, may be called the new diasporans, as distinct from the emigrants of the earlier eras, include the young, virile and talented men and women of Africa who tend to be closer and far more sensitive to the realities of industrialised economies than the African environment.

It is not my purpose in this chapter to challenge the strong commitment to higher education. Rather, it is my intention to analyse how the myths surrounding higher education as a *sine qua non* for development as embedded in the so-called theories of development hold promise for economic and social development in Africa in the twenty-first century. This chapter therefore looks more closely at the growing disjunction between higher education and the current status of Africa's socio-economic dynamism. The chapter addresses a number of questions. First, to provide a critical backdrop for the discussion of the role of education in nation building, I briefly give an overview of higher education policy in Africa. Second, I analyse the background of the culture of the African university. Third, I discuss the concept of development. Fourth, I provide an overview of theories of development that were adopted by African nations after independence from colonial masters. Fifth, I give a synopsis of the African diaspora and include a brief examination of the new wave of brain drain of African scholars, what I term the new diaspora, to the advanced industrialised world. I then propose some perspectives for the future. Finally, I critically analyse the role of higher education in the development of African nations and consider whether higher education is a true vehicle to social and economic development.

## 2. Higher Education Policy in Africa

Thinking about higher education policy and practice in Africa continues to be heavily influenced, if not dominated, by ideas about education as the key to national development and social reconstruction. During the 1960s, when most colonies became independent, governments of the newly independent countries began to establish undergraduate and college-type programs in all fields of education in response to the modernisation theory. Universities, especially as they developed in Africa, were similar to universities in advanced industrialised countries. These institutions have been deeply embedded in educational philosophies and ideologies whose purpose has been to train and sponsor privileged elites that would take over the realms of colonial administration.

Whereas a cursory examination of African nations will reveal that higher education has remained an area in which most countries maintain a strong commitment, it continues to fail to produce the desired results. Since independence from the colonial masters, despite capricious changes of ambivalent and periodically turbulent and disorderly political and economic environments, African nations continue to emphasise higher education as a vehicle for social and economic development. Education has thus become the last ditch defence of a debt-ridden Africa grappling with the crises of underdevelopment, unemployment, currency devaluations and continuing material dispossession. The search for new patterns and designs for social living is the common anxiety of African nations, and for many they continue to struggle with the enormous and complex socio-economic forces that reduce them to conditions of pensiveness and obscurity. But is there a chance that the rhetoric about human capital and modernisation theories can improve the social dynamism and economic development of African nations? The reality is that most African countries structure their universities to serve the interests of the former colonial powers and do not bear relevance to the problems of African countries.[1] As Smillie writes: "Many Third World universities were founded in the shadow of European affiliates, most pursue academic programs based on international standards and on perceptions relating more to the international than to domestic academic community."[2]

Educational policies do not seem to attempt to remedy the rapidly deteriorating economic situation in Africa with its corresponding devastating social consequences. Commodity markets continue to deteriorate, thus robbing African countries of adequate foreign exchange earnings to balance their trade and meet their debt-servicing obligations. Because of rocketing import prices, there is escalating cost of the development needs of the countries. Famine resulting from low agricultural output, particularly food production, is mainly due to primordial farming implements, lack of appropriate input, inadequate irrigation facilities and the lack of effective food preservation facilities. The limitations imposed upon education and training by the idea of education as handed down to African governments by the colonial administrations have failed to ensure a realistic balance between education on one hand and the development and socio-economic needs on the other.

From the point of view that Africa will come to realise equal values in human capital in terms of the large investments in higher education, the outcome is uncertain at best, and gloomy at worst, if the brain drain among the young and talented generation of Africans continues. Issues facing African countries today concern low productivity, poverty, better job opportunities, lack of effective health care, education-labour market mismatch, competitive global economy and equality of educational access. Although these issues are varied, assumptions about the characteristic failure of Western education to ensure a down-to-earth equilibrium between education, particularly higher education, on the one hand and the socio-economic development and employment needs on the other, the contradictions of Western education in relation to nation building remain in the background of the education and development debate. Understanding the impact of higher education on the accelerating process of Africa's brain drain is part and parcel of conceptualising Africa's social dynamism today. Assuming it away as a critical issue creates serious difficulties in interpreting nation building in Africa.

## 3. Background of the Culture of the African University

From its birth in twelfth century Italy and France to its colonisation of the modern developing world, the university's meaning and purpose have changed from period to period and from generation to generation.[3] However, the uniqueness of the university lies in its capacity to pass through many stages of growth and development, changing its form and purpose to suit its momentary and socio-political environment while preserving its culture. Like all human institutions, the university maintains a tenacious endurance over time with a stubborn resistance to change in spite of external pressures and internal adjustments.[4] Traditionally an elite institution, the university has a strong element in the pursuit of theoretical rationality and that anything practical is ultimately not an embodiment of worthy knowledge and rationality.[5] This idea of the university is rooted in the empiricist tradition that emphasises the detachment of the subject from the object as the key role in the progressive unfolding of knowledge.

By tradition, the university strives to remain protected from external interference and is therefore unwilling to break its cultural mysteriousness and behavioural systems built over time. Although the university has provided social mobility to previously disenfranchised groups, it continues to maintain some form of social differentiation that perpetuates its elitist system.[6]

The African university, like its counterpart in the advsnced developed world, has maintained a stubborn resistance to change in spite of its inability to meet the socio-economic demands of the nation states. The university strives to remain protected from interference from the local community because it is unwilling to break the cultural mystique and behavioural codes characteristic of universities in the advanced industrialised world. Set against this backdrop of academic culture, it is clear that at the frontiers of knowledge in African universities, the meanings ascribed to *the idea of education* are inextricably linked to models in Western thinking. There has been increasing recognition of the interaction between the questions produced in terms of Western economic models of development and solutions offered within the Western world. As Smillie writes,

> Many Third World universities were founded in the shadow of European affiliates, most pursue academic programs based on international standards and on perceptions relating more to the international than to the domestic academic community.[7]

Many writers have repeatedly alleged that because of their quest for modernity, universities in developing countries do not perform functions that are relevant to the national development of their countries.[8] For example, Saha claims that the universities in developing countries produce graduates in the sciences who, either do not understand, or are not dedicated to the solution of the problems of the Third World.[9]

4.    **Concept of Development**

The term *development* is an elusive concept with several meanings, lending itself to a contextual definition. That is to say, researchers define it in the actual context in which they use the term *development*. Some researchers use the terms *development* and *growth* interchangeably.[10] Others use words such as social change, evolution progress, advancement, and modernisation as synonyms of development only when they refer to underdeveloped countries or regions, and others use the term *development* to mean fundamental changes in social attitudes and institutions. Malchup concludes that in reference to developing countries, *economic development* means economic growth.[11] Therefore, the term *development* implies change in a specific direction that the researcher regards as potential and highly important to the welfare of society.[12] Some philosophers, scientists, social scientists, and planners are inclined to identify development with social structures found in countries that are highly industrialised and advanced in education, science and technology.[13] Some writers regard development as the process of changing a basically traditional society into a modern one. Harrison, for example, contends that development is the same as modernisation.[14]

Thus, it becomes apparent that in referring to development, most scholars emphasise scientific and technical education, capital-intensive investment, market economy and other western ideologies.[15] According to de Souza and Porter, industrialisation and advancement lead to economic growth but do not necessarily lead to development.[16] They contend that economic growth is not development unless it leads to the achievement of particular human goals. Development should go with the human goals that are related to balanced diet at all times, adequate medical care, opportunities for learning useful skills and for developing the mind. The development of a society is crucial in its impact on personal freedom, safety and equality, adequate housing, and employment opportunities. According to de Souza and Porter, the *idea of education* in Africa which does not seem to link up with traditional concepts beyond the narrow confines Western literacy, runs the risk of misunderstanding the social context within which to carry out effective development. As de Souza and Porter write, "The economic and social changes which have occurred in poor countries in the past two decades have been as much cause for despair as for hope for those who want to see these countries develop."[17] Thus, the meaning of the concept *development* is inextricably linked to the degree of emphasis a researcher places on the indicators of development.

The international community adopted the term *development* to describe the sequence of economic growth of the nations of the Third World. The developing nations and the international community now recognise the term as a multi-dimensional concept. A landmark for the definition of the term *development* was the resolution of the United Nations General Assembly during the proclamation of the Second United Nations Development Decade on January 1, 1971.[18] The UN declared the following elements are basic to development:

1) a minimum standard of living compatible with human dignity;
2) underpinned improvement of the well-being of the individual;
3) sharing of benefits by society at large;
4) more equitable distribution of wealth and income and wealth;

5) a greater degree of income security; and
6) the safeguard of the environment.

Although some of the indicators such as a "minimum standard of living compatible with human dignity" seem to be vague, it is clear that the United Nations' indicators comprise the whole gamut of a country's economic, social and cultural life. Therefore, one could conveniently refer to development in multi-dimensional terms. That is, one cannot measure development by using only economic growth or by any other exclusive indicator.[19] Accordingly, the term *development* may imply a condition of well-being for society as a whole.

## 5. Theoretical Perspectives on Development

Among the many perspectives on development, the modernisation and human capital theories supply an ample framework for educational objectives in developing countries.

A.  Modernisation Theory

Modernisation theory was the response scholars gave to nation building and institution building after World War II. The Western world became interested in modernisation when colonies in the Third World started advocating political independence. This interest was mainly for politicians of the West to demonstrate to the world that newly independent countries could sustain development if they adopted Western strategies.[20] Modernisation theory originated in the early 1960s mainly from the work of David McClelland, a social psychologist who attempts to explain the differences between societies in social and technological advancement.[21] McClelland asserts that some societies are more advanced than others because of differences in cultural and personality styles. According to McClelland, advancement is caused by the need for achievement. He claims that children can develop the need for achievement through literature that stresses the significance of self-help, competition and general extroverted behaviour. Therefore, societies that wish to encourage their young to become entrepreneurs can impart them with the values of the need for achievement at the right age. So, for McClelland, modernisation is closely linked with the acquisition of modern values.

The modernity scale of Alex Inkeles, an American sociologist, became widely used in the 1960s and 1970s. From their study of individual modernity in six developing countries, Inkeles and Smith provide a rationale for the modernisation theory stating that people are modernised through specific life experiences, particularly experiences that have been shaped around complex and bureaucratic organisations.[22] Inkeles and his followers believe that to modernise is to develop, and society cannot develop until the bulk of its population absorbs modern values that are created through certain social institutions such as family, school and factory. For them, modernisation is closely tied to industrialisation. Therefore, the basic assumption underlying the modernisation theory is that there is a direct causal link between five sets of variables in the process of modernisation, namely, modernising institutions, modern values, modern behaviour, modern society and economic development. In his volume, *The Stages of Economic Growth - A Non-Communist Manifesto*, Rostow identifies five stages of economic growth that lead to development; they are:

1) the traditional society;
2) the preconditions of take-off;
3) the take-off;
4) the drive to maturity; and
5) the age of high mass consumption.[23]

Rostow describes a traditional society as an agricultural-dependent society with limited access to science and technology. In a traditional society, religion and natural laws dictate the mode of production. There is virtually a lack of diversification in the economy. The means of production are controlled by a social hierarchy with family and clan affiliations playing a greater role in society. In traditional societies, political power is usually vested in landowners who maintain considerable influence on society members.

The preconditions for take-off stage are a transitional period to modernity, a period when a developing society becomes aware of the need for advancement. The society at this period introduces innovations in education and develops infrastructure such as banks and other economic establishments for capital mobilisation and the encouragement of investment opportunities. At this stage, the society evolves practices that broaden the scope of commerce internally and externally and encourages the establishment of modern manufacturing industries. Rostow views the third stage, the take-off, as the most critical period of the development process. He refers to this stage as the period of rapid industrial and technological growth. In this stage there is a shift from labour-intensive to capital-intensive techniques of production. The fourth stage, the drive to maturity stage, is a period of long sustained growth. It is a period when society modernises all economic activities through technology. The final stage, the age of high mass consumption, is characterised by a period of economic growth when society moves toward demanding durable consumer goods and services. Accordingly, for Rostow, development is unilinear and in order for traditional societies to develop, they have to change their economies, values and social structures.

Consequently, the common view among many modernisation theorists between the 1950 and the 1970s was that education was directly linked with socio-economic development. In the long quest for socio-economic development, governments identified higher education as the area that would reduce their dependence on advanced countries. Ironically, higher institutions been deeply embedded in educational philosophies and ideologies whose purpose was to train and sponsor privileged elites that would take over the realms of colonial administration.[24]

B.   Human Capital Theory

The human capital theory proposes that the most productive route to the development of any society depends on its population, that is, the human capital. In his address to the American Economic Association in 1960, Theodore Schultz declared that education was a productive investment and was not merely a form of consumption.[25] He maintained that apart from improving individual choices available to people, education provides the category of labour force required for industrial development and economic growth. In his book, *Investing in people - the economics of population quality*, Schultz identifies the acquired abilities of people as the most important economic resource available to societies. He maintains that human capital is decisive in improving the welfare of poor people throughout the world.[26]

In the 1960s, social scientists became interested in studies related to the economic value of investment in education. This interest was generated by the human capital theorists' notion that the most productive course to national development of any society lies in the advancement of its population, that is its human capital.[27] In other words, human capital theory contends that because an educated population is a productive population, education contributes directly to the growth of the national income of societies by enhancing the skills and productive abilities of employees.[28] Human capital theorists argue that economic growth and development should only take place when technology becomes more efficient and when societies utilise human resources in the use of technology. Human capital theorists assume that improved technology leads to greater production and that employees acquire the skills for the use of technology through formal education. Thus, when societies invest in education, they invest to increase the productivity of the population.

C.   Dependency Theory

Researchers trace the origins of dependency theory from Marx and Lenin. Marx's idea of the exploitation of the proletariat by the bourgeois class and Lenin's concept of imperialism are used by dependency theorists to describe the process whereby capitalism dominates and exploits the poor countries. Dependency theory has its origins in the

1960s through the writings of scholars who were particularly concerned over the persistent economic crisis of Latin America countries. They reject the idea of modernisation theory that development would occur by exposing the Third World to the modern values of industrialised countries. Instead they argue that the persistent poverty in the Third World countries is caused by exposure to the economic, political and social influences of industrialised countries. Dependency theorists also assert that the growth of industrialised countries in the world today leads to the concurrent underdevelopment of those countries whose economic surplus the rich countries exploit.[29] Therefore, given time, poor countries would develop, but as long as they are subjected to the exploitation of the rich countries, their poverty would persist.

Andre Gunder Frank, one of the major proponents of the dependency theory is closely associated with the view that the persistent poverty of the Third World is an image of its dependency.[30] According to Frank, merchants and colonial powers forced Third World countries to become exporters of primary products to satisfy the raw material needs of the imperial powers. In doing so, these merchants and colonial powers incorporated the Third World elite into their system of exploitation. The elites became mere intermediaries between the rich merchant buyers and the poor producers. Thus, the elites' lifestyles were increasingly bound to and seriously dependent on the activities of the economic elite in industrialised countries. While the elite in the Third World enjoy a high standard of living from their relationship with the advanced countries, the masses experience persistent deprivation as the elite take their surplus production from them in the local rural region and transfer the products abroad. Frank terms this form of dependency *lumpenbourgeoisie* and *lumpendevelopment*. According to Frank, dependency relationships occur when the elite of the poor countries bear attitudes, values and interests consistent with those in the wealthy countries. The elites, *lumpenbourgeoisie*, are principal agents of the dependency relationship.

Similarly, Santos writes, "Dependence is a conditioning situation in which the economies of one group of countries are conditioned by the development and expansion of others."[31] According to Santos, dependent countries remain in a state of helplessness that causes them to be both backward and exploited. This means that the rich countries dominate and exploit the poor countries by transferring resources from the poor countries to their countries through colonial or neo-colonial relationships. For Santos, dependence is a condition of an "international division of labour that allows industrial development to take place in some countries while restricting it in others, whose growth is conditioned by and subjected to the power centres of the world."[32]

Accordingly, in contrast to modernisation theory, dependency theory highlights the social, political, cultural and economic relationships both between and within societies. The underdevelopment of a country or region is linked to the development of another country or outside region. Therefore dependency theory assumes that the world is divided into core and peripheral countries, dominated by a capitalist economic network, whereby the rich core countries exploit the poor peripheral ones.

## 6. The African Diaspora

The term African diaspora is simply the dispersal and settlement of peoples of Africa beyond the African continent. According to Shepperson, the term *African diaspora* came into existence in the late 1950s and 1960s at the same time that African nations were seeking independence from their colonial masters.[33] Shepperson argues "the expression *African diaspora* began to be used increasingly by writers and thinkers who were concerned with the status and prospects of persons of African descent around the world as well as at home."[34] Okpewho states that the "*diaspora* represents a global space, a worldwide web, that accounts as much for the mother continent as for wherever in the world her offspring may have been driven by the unkind forces of history." [35]

*Diaspora* is essentially a Greek word for dispersal as maintained in the *Book of Deuteronomy (28:25)*.[36] According to Shepperson, "…until [diaspora] began to have the adjective *African* or *black* attached to it, was used largely for the scattering abroad of the Jews."[37] The genesis of the term *African diaspora* was at the First International Congress of Negro Writers and Artists in Paris in 1956.[38] Okpewho designates three phases as precursors for the African Diaspora in the New World: The first phase was the period of the labour imperative. This period characterised the source of the diaspora of enslavement when slaves were transported from Africa from the 16$^{th}$ century onwards to exploit their labour in building the New World. This was a period of wasted brain drain. The second phase was the period of the territorial imperative or the era of colonialism. The Monroe Doctrine in 1823 and the founding of Liberia became a precursor for the scramble for, and the partition of Africa. The third phase is termed the extractive imperative, a period when Africa's natural resources became the focus of the imperial powers.[39]

In contrast to the labour imperative that was wasted brain drain, the 20$^{th}$ century labour movements, labour globalisation, were characterised by voluntary brain drain.[40] It is here that I discern a definite break between the old and the new African diaspora. For while the aforementioned imperatives were precursors to the African presence in the New World, the new African diaspora stemmed in part from the results of the 20$^{th}$ century labour globalisation.

## 7. The New Diaspora in the Context of Dependency Theory

The migration of African immigrants to the United States since the 1980s has been influenced by two reasons. The first is the changing immigration policies of colonial powers that hitherto had historical and political ties with African countries.[41] Colonial ties encouraged early migration of Africans to the United Kingdom, France and Belgium until these countries started experiencing a long period of economic recession that made them to implement restrictive immigration policies that debarred Africans from entering without visas. The second is the more relaxed policies of the United States towards immigrants from developing countries. By 1965, the U.S. introduced the family reunification and refugee law that were greatly in favour of African immigrants.[42] Since then there has been a steady influx of Africans into the New World.

The 1980 U.S. Census indicated that of the 225,000 Africans in the United States, 60 per cent were white, 29 per cent were black and 11 percent identified as other.[43] The 1990 Census indicated that of about one half million Africans in the United States, 47 percent were black, 44 percent were white and 9 percent were classified as other. According to the 2000 U.S. Census, about one million Africans now live in the United States. Most of these African immigrants are highly educated and skilled. According to Djamba, the 1980 and 1990 censuses indicated that there were more people among black Africans age 16 and older with college education than white Africans and Native Blacks. For example, in 1980, about 88 percent of adult black male and 66 percent of black female African immigrants in the U.S. had college education compared to 79 percent for males and 63 percent for females in 1990.[44] The 2000 census also indicated that black African immigrants are the most educated of all the immigrants in the U.S. with 49 percent holding bachelor degrees.[45]

Many of the African students offered financial support for graduate studies overseas do not return to their home countries. Rather, the majority constitutes a brain drain that finds placement in the labour market of their host countries. Given the current process of migration of African scholars to the advanced countries, dependency, rather than nation building provides an arena in which to view the role of higher education in Africa.

Ironically, the technocratic achievements of the human capital and modernisation theories have proved to be their chief sources of weaknesses and vulnerability as well. Higher education in developing countries produces experts who look to academics in the industrialised countries as their reference group, and as a result emulate them to the extent of taking higher paid jobs overseas while their home countries lose the very talents that have been inappropriately educated.[46] The number of African academics who receive education and training in the advanced countries and the proportion migrating to these countries to pursue professional careers is steadily growing. This accelerating process has been termed the brain drain. For want of any better terminology I call this trend, the new diaspora that comprises the young and talented cream of African academics who otherwise could have been national elites to set African nations on the path of economic and social development.

## 8. A Perspective with a Future Orientation

Dependency theorists, with their neo-Marxist background accept the notion that even in advanced capitalist societies, education helps to perpetuate inequalities by serving the interests of those in power. Historically, the ideological and institutional underpinnings of schooling have geared towards expanding opportunities for the upper classes rather than the children of the middle and working classes. The dependency school contends that since schooling in the former colonial societies has been imported from the Western world, it only continues to benefit the dominant social group as it did for the colonial system as a whole. Therefore, many neo-Marxists (including the dependency school) believe that in most developing countries, schools are merely a new form of colonialism and imperialism. They argue that by adopting selection procedures and curricula structures of former colonial powers, schools continue to serve the interests of the elite of these former powers.

What then are the prospects of higher education as a vehicle for development under these inauspicious circumstances? In contrast to development strategies based on modernisation, developing countries need to adopt Marxist or neo-Marxist strategies of development to direct educational reforms and outcomes towards restructuring of the school systems to conform to the needs of society. Educational reforms should initially attempt to eliminate privilege and elitism in the school system. We can safely attribute the movement of the most talented young men and women to the advanced capitalist countries to the cultural dislocation of higher education from the traditional societies of developing countries. The common ethos of this movement is that Africa is losing the best of its human capital to the developed world. The devastating effects of this brain drain can be termed as a neo-colonial domination of the developing countries.

An argument made, often forcefully and convincingly by social theorists is that universities in developing countries would almost certainly fail if their particular goals are not specified carefully and tailored to suit their culture and environment.[47] If the present trend of immigration of trained academics from the developing countries to advanced countries continues, we may expect a continuing lopsided growth and increasing immigration of people to the advanced countries. This represents a vicious cycle of loss of human capital that can further slow the attainment of nation building objectives.

However, socio-economic development is only one aspect according to which one can access the role of universities in nation building. Although the socio-economic considerations are certainly important, there are other intangible aspects of the contributions of higher education to society that cannot be measured quantitatively. One of these is that the African university needs to become closely related to its local environment and draw inspiration from it because "in [the local environment] are embedded the roots of African culture and civilisation-worldview, values, customs, and traditions, creative works, knowledge, skills, and technology."[48] The African university must therefore aim at preserving the traditional environment and enhancing pride in Africa's cultural heritage.

For education to act as a propeller of socio-economic growth, there is the need for the following:

1) agricultural education institutions should pool their resources together and improve upon the traditional systems of farming;
2) adequate links between universities and the job market, offering appropriate training for skills needed in the labour market;
3) a balance between enrolments in disciplines that would act as the engine of growth;
4) eradication of gender inequalities by encouraging the enrolment of women in higher education;
5) making universities less costly by adopting higher priorities in educational policy planning;
6) promotion of international cooperation;
7) effective links to the cultural and social environment to enhance nation building;
8) emphasis on the institutional management that would lead the nation on the path to development; and
9) a program for coordinated research by African universities to build up a store of expert knowledge, experience and know-how in fields relevant to nation building.

## 9. Conclusion

The debate on socio-economic development of African countries has for too long centred on a stale ideological debate between the competing virtues of Western strategies and traditional forms. Can we learn the lessons of the past and shape a more compassionate strategy for the future development of Africa? The human capital theorists' idea of education as a vehicle for economic growth and national development that has dominated educational planning and development strategies of governments in African countries since the 1960s and 1970s has been demonstrably weak on fulfilling the ideals of socio-economic development and nation building. Both the human capital and modernisation theories have made hundreds of thousands of educated and talented Africans vulnerable to a "modernisation temptation" that has produced a mass influx of these men and women to industrialised countries. While I do not question the contribution of education to development, I question whether education in its present form can contribute to social and political equality that is considered important to the continued advancement of developing countries. In Africa, where the models of universities have been adopted from advanced industrialised countries, there is a pressing need for devising a strategy that could utilise traditional resources in greater harmony and cooperation with Western strategies.

Paradoxically enough, each model of development adopted by governments in Africa contains within itself also the seeds of self-destruction. The forces unleashed by the very process of higher education have managed to perpetuate a dependency that forms the basis of the new African diaspora. Given patterns of excessive reliance on primary production and the cultural emphasis placed on agriculture in developing countries, one would expect symbolic and policy commitment to economic growth via agricultural education. However, higher education in agriculture in developing countries has long placed undue emphasis on academic courses and programs. Sherman and others have repeatedly alleged that because of their modernity, universities in developing countries do not perform functions that are relevant to their national development.[49] The development of appropriate and cheap technology for food cultivation and methods of preservation and conservation should be a priority for higher education institutions. Since farming implements imported from the advanced countries have proved inappropriate and expensive, agricultural education should equip graduates with the expertise to work in collaboration with the local craftsmen to develop implements that are suitable to tropical soil conditions and to the needs of the farmers.

Fagerlind and Saha contend that a dialectical process occurs between education and society. Simply put, education is a product of society and at the same time, acts continually upon society to effect change. Each of the principal dimensions of development, such as the economic, political and social dimensions acts upon education, and education in turn acts upon each of these dimensions. So, the contribution of education to the development process depends upon the nature of the other dimensions of development in a given society at a particular time.[50]

Saha has viewed the process of modernisation essentially in terms of expansion of individual benefits through higher education as compared with societal benefits that are found in traditional cultures.[51] While some may negatively interpret the brain drain in Africa, Saha sees it as a source of growth and development as many of the emigrants continue to maintain contacts with the academics of their home countries and sometimes return to those countries to contribute to national development.[52] Furthermore, for a global economy, the brain drain constitutes a free dissemination of knowledge and information in the marketplace of ideas, a *sine qua non* that makes the academic professional an international profession.

Several studies have demonstrated the relationships between education and economic levels of development among societies.[53] In a study conducted in 44 countries using the human capital approach, Psacharopoulos conducted a survey on the rates of return to educational investment. He found that first, primary education reveals the highest social and private returns. Secondly, private returns are higher than social returns, particularly at the university level. Thirdly, all rates of return to investment in education exceed the rates of return in alternative investment in capital. And finally, developing countries' rates of returns to investment in education are higher than those of industrialised countries at comparable levels.[54]

There is no doubt that the evidence about the efficacy of higher education in nation building is convincing. However the actual mechanisms that should make higher education meaningful and result-oriented are lacking. One area from where African universities can benefit is the need to emphasise the sharing of knowledge and ideas between and among the universities through periodical inter-regional expert group meetings where universities can share results of research projects, project successes and failures and lessons learned from various project implementations. Thus the myths surrounding higher education as a *sine qua non* for development can be seen in the light of how new techniques reshape culturally defined methods of livelihood in Africa.

## Notes

[1] Mary Sherman, "The University in Modern Africa: Toward the Twenty-First Century," *The Journal of Higher Education* 61(4) (1990): 363-385.

[2] Ian Smillie, *No Condition Permanent: Pump-Priming Ghana's Industrial Revolution* (London : Intermediate Technology Publications, 1986), 65.

[3] Harold Perkin, "The Historical Perspective," in *Perspectives on Higher Education: Eight Disciplinary and Comparative Views*, ed. Burton R. Clark (Bekeley: University of California Press, 1984), 16-55.

[4] Ibid

⁵ Parker Palmer, Learning Communities: Reweaving the Culture of Disconnection," *Washington Center News*, Spring 2000, 34-35. Palmer's view clearly summarizes the reasons for the detachment of universities from their natural environments. Our aggrandizement of Western style of knowing as the ultimate source of the best knowledge, authority and legitimacy present some real problems for the future of education in Africa.

⁶ Philip Altbach, "Patterns in Higher Education Development: Toward Year 2000," in *Emergent issues in education: Comparative perspectives,* ed. Robert F. Arnove et al., (Albany: State University of New York Press, 1992), 39-55.

⁷ Smillie, 65.

⁸ Lawrence J. Saha, "Universities and National Development – Issues and Problems in Developing countries," Prospects, 21(2) (1991): 248-257. For more insightful analysis of higher education in developing countries, see Sherman, 363-385; Altbach, 39-55.

⁹ Ibid, 253.

¹⁰ Fritz Machlup Education and Economic Growth (Lincoln: University of Nebraska Press, 1970).

¹¹ Ibid

¹² Ingemar Fagerlind & Lawrence J. Saha, Education and National Development: A Comparative Perspective (2$^{nd}$ edition) Exeter: BPCC Wheatons Ltd., 1989)

¹³ Walt W. Rostow The stages of Economic Growth – A non Communist Manifesto (3$^{rd}$ edition). New York: Cambridge University Press, 1990).

¹⁴ David Harrison The sociology of modernization and development (London: Unwin Hyman, 1988).

¹⁵ Shamsul Huq, Education, Manpower and Development in South and Southeast Asia (New York: Praeger Publishers, 1975).

¹⁶ Anthony R. De Souza and Philip W. Porter, The Underdevelopment and Modernization of the Third World (Washington, DC: Association of American Geographers, 1974).

¹⁷ Ibid, 4.

¹⁸ UN International Development Strategy: United Nations Action Program of the General Assembly for Second UN Development Decade. New York: The United Nations, 1974).

¹⁹ Gunnar Myrdal, *Asian drama: An Inquiry into the Poverty of Nations* New York: Random House, 1972).

²⁰ Andrew Webster, *Introduction to the sociology of development* (Basingstoke: Macmillan, 1990).

²¹ David C. McClelland, *The Achieving Society* (New York: van Nostrand, 1961).

[22] Alex Inkeles & David H. Smith, *Becoming modern: Individual change in six developing countries* (Cambridge: Harvard University Press, 1974).

[23] For a more comprehensive analysis of the stages of economic development, see Rostow's Stages of Economic Growth (3rd Edition).

[24] It is not surprising that African universities bear vestiges of advanced industrialized countries because most of the local faculty members acquire their training overseas and also many university teaching positions are held by so-called experts from the advanced industrialized countries.

[25] Theodore. W. Schultz, "Education and economic growth" in N. B. Henry (Ed.), *Social Forces Influencing American Education,* (Chicago: University of Chicago Press, 1961). Shultz is considered the proponent of the human capital theory.

[26] Theodore W. Schultz, *Investing In People*: *The Economics of Population Quality*, (Berkeley: The University of California Press, 1981).

[27] Gary S. Becker, *Human capital: A theoretical and Empirical Analysis, with Special Reference to Education,* (3rd edition) (Chicago: University of Chicago Press, 1993).

[28] George Psacharopoulos, *Higher Education in Developing Countrie: A Cost Benefit Analysis.* World Bank Staff Papers #44. (Washington, DC: World Bank, 1980).

[29] Ivan Head, *On a Hinge of History: The Mutual Vulnerability of South and North.* (Toronto: University of Toronto Press, 1991) gives a very lucid account of how advanced countries exploit the developing countries.

[30] Andre G. Frank, Lumpenbourgeoisie: Lumpendevelopment – Dependence, Class, and Politics in Latin America, (New York: Monthly Review Press, 1972).

[31] Tano Santos 'The crisis of development theory and the problem of development in Latin America', in *Underdevelopment and Development*, ed. Henry Bernstein, (Harmondsworth: Penguin, 1973) 57-80.

[32] Ibid, 76-77.

[33] George Shepperson, "African diaspora: Concept and context," in *Global Dimensions of the Africa Ddiaspora* (2nd edition) ed. Joseph E. Harris (Washington, DC: Howard University Press, 1993), 41-49. In this article, Shepperson provides a lucid analysis of the genesis of the African diaspora.

[34] Ibid, 41.

[35] Isidore Okpewho, "Introduction," in *The African diaspora: African origins and new world identities*, ed. Isidore Okpewho et al., (Bloomington, IN: Indian University Press, 1999), ix-xxviii

[36] See the Old Testament in the Holy Bible
[37] Shepperson, 41.
[38] Ibid
[39] Okpewho provides a cogent discussion of the phases of the African diaspora.
[40] The labour imperative period was characterized by slavery and the slave trade.
[41] Yanyi K. Djamba "African Immigrants in the United States: A Socio-demographicPprofile in Comparison to Native Blacks. *Journal of Asian and African Studies*, 34 (2) (1999): 210-304.
[42] Ibid
[43] Ibid
[44] Ibid: Djamba provides a cogent analysis of socio-demographic profiles of African immigrants in the U.S.
[45] 2000 U.S. Census.
[46] Saha
[47] See Sherman, and Saha
[48] See Sherman, 371.
[49] Saha 248-257.
[50] See Fagerlind and Saha,
[51] Saha
[52] Ibid
[53] Katharina Michaelowa, Returns to education in low-income countries: Evidence for Africa. Paper presented at the annual meeting of the Committee on Developing Countries of the German Economic Association (June 30, 200). Hamburg Institute for International Economics.
[54] See Psacharopoulos.

# Bibliography

Altbach, Philip G. "Patterns in higher education development: Toward year 2000." In *Emergent issues in education: Comparative perspectives* edited by Robert F. Arnove et al., 39-55. Albany: State University of New York Press, 1992.

Becker, Gary S. *Human Capital: A Theoretical and Empirical Analysis, with Special Reference to Education ($3^{rd}$ edition).* Chicago : The University of Chicago Press, 1993.

De Souza, Anthony R. and Porter, Philip. W. *The Underdevelopment and Modernization of the Third World.* Washington, DC: Association of American Geographers, 1974.

Djamba, Yanyi K. "African immigrants in the United States: A Socio-Demographic Profile in Comparison to Native Blacks," *Journal of Asian and African Studies,* 34 (2) (1999): 210-304.

Fagerlind, Ingemar & Saha, Lawrence J. *Education and National Development: A Comparative Perspective* (2$^{nd}$ ed.). Exeter: BPCC Wheatons Ltd., 1989.

Frank, Andre G. *Lumpenbourgeoisie: Lumpendevelopment – Dependence, Class, and Politics in Latin America.* New York: Monthly Review Press, 1972.

Harrison, David. *The sociology of modernization and development.* London: Unwin Hyman, 1988.

Head, Ivan L. *On a Hinge of History: The Mutual Vulnerability of South and North.* Toronto: University of Toronto Press, 1991.

Huq, Shamsul. *Education, Manpower and Development in South and Southeast Asia.* New York: Praeger, 1975.

Inkeles, Alex & Smith, David H. *Becoming Modern: Individual Change in Six Developing Countries.* Cambridge: Harvard University Press, 1974.

Machlup, Fritz. *Education and Economic Growth.* Lincoln: University of Nebraska Press, 1970.

McClelland, David. C. *The Achieving Society.* New York: van Nostrand, 1961.

Michaelowa Katharina, *Returns to education in low-income countries: Evidence for Africa.* Paper presented at the annual meeting of the Committee on Developing Countries of the German Economic Association Hamburg Institute for International Economic, 30 June, 2000.

Myrdal, Gunnar. *Asian Drama: An Inquiry into the Poverty of Nations.* New York: Random House, 1972.

Okpewho Isidore. "Introduction." In: *The African diaspora: African origins and new world identities,* edited by Isidore Okpewho et al., ix-xxviii. Bloomington (IN): Indian University Press, 1999.

Psacharopoulos, George. *Higher Education in Developing Countries – A Cost Benefit Analysis. World Bank Staff Papers #44.* Washington, DC: World Bank, 1980.

Rostow, Walt W. *The Stages of Economic Growth – A Non Communist Manifesto* (3$^{rd}$ edition). New York: Cambridge University Press, 1990.

Saha, Lawrence J. "Universities and National Development – Issues and Problems in Developing Countries," *Prospects*, 21(2) (1991): 248-257.

Santos, Tano. "The Crisis of Development Theory and the Problem of Development in Latin America." In *Underdevelopment and Development*, edited by Henry Bernstein, 55-80. Harmondsworth: Penguin, 1973.

Shepperson, George. "African Diaspora: Concept and Context." In *Global Dimensions of the African Diaspora* (2nd edition), edited by Joseph E. Harris, 41-49. Washington, DC: Howard University Press, 1993.

Sherman, Mary. A. B. "The University in Modern Africa – Toward the Twenty-First Century," *The Journal of Higher Education*, 61(4) (1990): 363-385.

Schultz, Theodore W. "Nobel Lecture: The Economics of Being Poor," *Journal of Political Economy*, 88(4) (1980): 639-652.

Schultz, Theodore W. *Investing In people – TheEeconomics of Population Quality*. Berkeley: University of California Press, 1981.

UN International Development Strategy: United Nations Action Program of the General Assembly for Second UN Development Decade. New York: The United Nations. Wageningen: Pudoc, 1971.

Webster, Andrew, *Introduction to the Sociology of Development.* Basingstoke: Macmillan, 1990.

# CHAPTER FIVE

## From 'Education' to 'Educability': The Changing Nature of the Research/Teaching Nexus in the Modern University

### *Tom Claes*

**Abstract**
Traditionally, the research/teaching nexus is seen as the heart of the modern university. The basic argument of this chapter is that recent changes in the type of preferred research and the way in which this research is carried out has some fundamental consequences for the identity of this modern university. In this chapter I will focus mainly on the European level and on the policies and trends that have shaped the university landscape from the last decades of the 20th century onwards. I start by giving an overview of some of these developments. Focusing on European trends allows us to transcend national perspectives. I will then continue by answering three, interrelated, questions: What are the main characteristics of the new economic rationale for the university?; What are the emerging dominant types of university research that accompany this new rationale?; and How does this influence the research and teaching mission of the university? I will conclude this chapter by raising some questions and concerns regarding this modern university, suggesting that this modern university faces some problems that threaten its traditional identity and which could very well lead to the end of the traditional university.

Key Words: Education; Educability; Research/Teaching Nexus; European Union; Higher Education; Entrepreneurial University; Innovation.

1. **Introduction**
The modern university operates within a larger social, cultural, intellectual, political and economic context. The contemporary university, traditionally taken as a free haven for disinterested research and education, becomes more and more embedded within an *economic project*, tailored to the needs of individual nation-states and regions. Scarce financial resources and the need to promote economic growth deeply influence the dominant models in science policy, and hence the ways of financing and organising the university.

Modern models of (economic) innovation and of the relation between university, industry, and government like the *Triple Helix model*, together with recent models and typologies of knowledge production, for example the models of Stokes, Gibbons and 'Jeffersonian science,' provide an ideological and intellectual justification for a fundamental transformation of the modern university. According to some, the changes that result from this could very well have some serious consequences for the university, resulting, for example, in the creation of two distinct types of institutions, one focusing on research, one on teaching, thereby effectively destroying the very idea of a university. Others welcome the new structures and possibilities and argue that the changes could lead to the disappearance of an outdated model of the university, and result in the emergence of types of universities that are better tuned to the needs of society.

Traditionally, the research/teaching nexus is seen as the heart of the modern university. The basic argument of this chapter is that recent changes in the type of preferred research and the way in which this research is carried out has some fundamental consequences for the identity of this modern university. In this chapter I will focus mainly on the European level and on the policies and trends that have shaped the university landscape from the last decades of the 20th Century onwards. I start by giving an overview of some of these developments. Zooming out to European trends allows us to transcend national perspectives. I will then continue by answering three, interrelated, questions: What are the main characteristics of the new economic rationale for the university?; What are the emerging dominant types of university research that accompany this new rationale?; and How does this influence the research and teaching mission of the university? I will conclude this chapter by raising some questions and concerns regarding this modern university, suggesting that this modern university faces some problems that threaten its traditional identity, which could very well lead to the end of the traditional university.

## 2. A New Economy, A New Policy: A European Perspective

Ever since the beginnings of what later would become the European Union, the political agendas behind the drive and process towards unionisation have been heavily shaped by *economic motives and considerations*. During the eighties and the early years of the nineties, this economic imperative crystallised into the creation of a single market. Some important dates and publications that mark this process are, e.g. the *Treaty of Rome* (1957), Delor's and Lord Cockfield's *Completing the internal Market: White Paper from the Commission to the European Council* (1985), *The Single European Act* (1986, ratification in 1987) in which a European research and technology policy was advocated, and the *Treaty of Maastricht* (1992) in which education was introduced in a Union Treaty. By 1993, the internal market was largely completed. Recently this process has been crowned by the introduction of the Euro. From the mid-nineties onwards this economic imperative was further translated into policies regarding the need for innovation, the creation of an information society, and the reorganisation of higher education and research.

In 1995 the European Commission published the *Green Paper on Innovation,* anchoring one of the new buzzwords firmly in the top of awareness of politicians, entrepreneurs, social partners, and of the general public. Successful innovation was seen as one of the key factors in economic growth, and research, development and the use of new technologies were seen as key elements in innovation. In the green paper, ideas were scouted on how to overcome the weaknesses in Europe's research and industrial base - as perceived earlier in the 1993 White Paper "Growth, Competitiveness, Employment. The Challenges and Ways Forward into the 21$^{st}$ Century" - such as the proportionally and comparatively low investments in research and technological development and the lack of co-ordination at various levels of the research and technological development activities (RTD). Finally yet importantly, the European Commission wanted to boost an alleged comparatively limited capacity to convert scientific breakthroughs and technological achievements into industrial and commercial successes.

These ideas, of course, were hardly new, nor innovative themselves, but the adoption of the principle of innovation as one of the central concerns of the EU and the ensuing actions, programs and legislation have had a profound influence on the European universities, research institutes of all kinds, and on Higher Education in general. When "innovation is at the heart of the spirit of enterprise"[1] and the management of scientific breakthroughs and technological achievements into industrial and commercial successes is considered to be one of the central levers of innovation, then the management of the producers of innovative knowledge and technologies becomes paramount. The focus on research and technology within the economic context of innovation and development fundamentally influences how one of the traditional missions of the university, *i.e.* scientific research, is organised, financed and carried out.

The same 1993 *White Paper on Growth, Competitiveness, Employment* that laid the basis for the future focus on innovation, paved the way for another crucial development in EU policy affecting universities, research institutes and Higher Education: the propagation of the Union as an Information Society. These plans were further elaborated in so-called Bangeman-report *Europe and the Global Information Society* (1994), prepared for the June 1994 meeting of the European Council in Corfu and in the June 1994 Action Plan "Europe's Way to the Information Society". In 1996 the European Commission published a communication in which some priority concerns were identified, for example, the need for enhancing the knowledge base and supporting the vision of a *Global Research Village.* A newly installed *Information Society Forum* stated that education and training should be quickly revised so that learning institutions would be more responsive to the need of the emerging industries.

Ideas like these blend in with the analyses and proposed guidelines made in the 1995 *White Paper on Education and Training* in which the main effects of the information society and internationalisation were taken to be the transformation of the nature of work and the organisation of production. The White Paper called for an adaptation not only to new technical tools but also to changes in working conditions and for an increase in skill and qualification levels in order to maintain the European social model. Although the White Paper and subsequent communications warn us not to think in purely economic terms, and to underscore the importance of personal fulfilment of the individual as one of the essential objectives of education and training, the Commission clearly notes that the move towards the knowledge society has important economic consequences as well and that these have to be addressed by means of education and training. According to the Commission the European Union should therefore continually strengthen its competitiveness by drawing on what is called its main asset, namely its capacity to generate and use knowledge with the aid of the great potential of its labour force.[2]

By the end of the nineties two important projects were well underway: the creation of a *European Research Area* (ERA) and of a *European Higher Education Area* - a Union of Research and a Union of Knowledge under the *aegis* of a what could be called a Union of Economic Innovation. These and other projects were even more closely knitted together during the Lisbon European Council of 23 and 14 March 2000 where an agreement was reached on a new strategic goal for the Union: "to become the most competitive and dynamic knowledge-based economy in the world, capable of sustainable economic growth with more and better jobs and greater social cohesion."[3]

## 3. A New Economic Rationale for the University
A. The Entrepreneurial University

These European trends mimic and reinforce trends on the level of the individual EU member states. The university has become one of the key players within the national innovation systems. In order to be able to play this role properly, the university has to adapt itself to this changing environment, and adjust its traditional missions of teaching, research and service to society accordingly.

Henry Etzkowitz and Loet Leydesdorff argue that the modern university is currently undergoing a *second* revolution. The first revolution occurred when the research mission was added to the traditional educational mission. A second revolution is now well underway and it fundamentally influences the way in which this first revolution is carried further. We witness the creation of the entrepreneur-university encompassing a so-called *third mission* of economic development in addition to research and teaching, and the emergence of an entrepreneurial culture within academia. This culture is by no means limited to a special class of universities that focus on applied research or professional disciplines. According to Etzkowitz and Leydesdorff the introduction of entrepreneurialism is a global phenomenon. The concept of the entrepreneurial university, so they argue, envisions an academic structure and function that is revised through the alignment of economic development with research and teaching as academic missions.[4]

The two traditional missions of the university - research and teaching - are becoming more and more tuned to the third mission: service to society, in this case, contributing to economic prosperity by playing a central role within the innovation system. This is sometimes referred to as 'the new social contract' for the university. However, it would be wrong envisaging the contribution of the university to this third mission as merely turning out more codified public knowledge based on its traditional function of doing basic research.

B. Knowledge, Research and Innovation

In the modern economy, an increasing amount of services, production processes and products are knowledge-based. Public knowledge, emanating from publicly financed research institutions and universities, plays an important role, substantiating the claim that public science is a driving force behind high technology. However, research carried out in collaboration between public institutions and private companies is crucial as well.[5] All this points towards the conclusion that the so-called *knowledge-society* or *information-society* is derivative of and ministerial to the knowledge-economy. The key to understanding the role of the university in the knowledge-society, and of the recent changes within the university, lies in understanding how this knowledge-economy works and how knowledge and innovation are linked.

There is no shortage of theories trying to model the role of research and knowledge within the innovation-process.[6] They all point, however, towards the same conclusion. The older linear model of innovation in which research was thought to generate development, hence production and finally marketing, had to be abandoned and it is recognised that ideas for innovation can stem from many sources.[7]

The traditional view on the possible contribution of universities and research institutions to the economy had to be adjusted. In this post-war view universities and publicly funded research institutes were seen as producers of chunks of codified public knowledge, published in journals accessible to all, not intentionally tailored to economic usefulness, but free, however, for the industry to use as the basis for innovation. This informational view of knowledge has been replaced by an evolutionary view on the economic relevance of publicly funded research.[8]

The most important contribution of academic research to the economy is not the article or book in which ideas are set forth - this accounts only for some 25% of the economic benefits of publicly funded research. The main economic benefits of basic research are not research findings directly applicable in a range of sectors, but background knowledge, research skills, instruments and methods that yield economic benefits over a much broader range of sectors.[9]

The links between science and industry have become both intensified and diversified. Turning away from codified knowledge as the main economic output of research institutes and universities has brought the training function of the university centre stage, for "smart people are the most critical resource to any economy and especially to the rapidly growing knowledge-based economy"[10] and networks between the all the economically relevant agents become crucial.[11]

In a knowledge-based economy, universities (and other research institutes), industry and government become increasingly intertwined, resulting in what Leydesdorff and Etzkowitz have called the Triple Helix of university-industry-government relations. This emerging knowledge infrastructure is constantly in flux and the,

> emerging system rests like a hyper-network on the networks on which it builds (such as the disciplines, the industries, and the national governments), but the knowledge-economy transforms 'the ship while a storm is raging on the open sea'.[12]

C. Towards an Economic Rationale

Scientific research, knowledge and skills, together with favourable economic conditions, are considered the most important long term levers for creating the knowledge economy and generating wealth. All this has led to the formulation of a new rationale and policy for managing the national and international science systems.[13] Within this system, universities are rapidly becoming the central agents of the public sector research system (PSR), while, at the same time, the role of dedicated research institutes is decreasing. The main targets of the policy mechanisms developed to manage the science base and the PSR are new procedures of evaluation, enhancing co-ordination between the different elements and layers of the system, prioritisation, the convergence of management practices and linking PSR with wider economic needs.[14]

Governments can influence university research and behaviour either *directly* or *indirectly*. Direct influence on what is researched and how, would seem to go against one of the central pillars of academic research: academic freedom. It would seem to contradict the historical and still growing autonomy of the university. However, a growing institutional autonomy does not always contradict and indeed often *indirectly* leads to linking university research and teaching to the economic and social environment even more.[15] One of the most important policy mechanisms to ensure this adaptation of the university to the needs of the innovation-driven economy, while at the same time respecting its autonomy, is the restructuring of the basic financing mechanisms of the university. It comes as no surprise then, that from the eighties onwards we witness a massive structural change in the financing systems of universities and in the internal allocation mechanisms of funds.[16]

Jane Millar and Jacqueline Senker recently reported that these changes have led to the dominance of the so called dual support system for research.[17] A dual support system is a split system in which core university funding and funding for research projects are allocated by separate institutions. Generally, the core university funds only cover some 25% of the amount required for research. Universities therefore have to obtain the additional funds from a variety of sources. This has led to an expansion of the share of competitive research funds to core funds. These competitive research funds are in most part contract-based and they are highly efficient in *indirectly* aligning university research with the societal and economic needs referred to earlier.[18] This leads to what Aldo Geuna has called a new rationale for university research funding, characterised by a competitive approach to university research behaviour and funding.[19]

The effects of the growing importance of competitive research financing are divers and legio, and include, among others, concentration of research means and agendas, increasing focus on collaborative research, growing importance of intellectual ownership and patents, higher researcher mobility, casualisation of the research work-force and spill-over effects on teaching and the dissemination of knowledge. One of the more salient effects is a heightened institutional pressure concerning available financial means.

4. **Emerging Dominant Types of University Research**

Changes in the structure for financing research influence what type of research is carried out. Salter and Martin state that a "new rationale for public funding of basic research also needs to take into account the debate about the changing nature of research."[20]

The nature of the dominant university research has changed from *basic, curiosity driven* to *use inspired,* from long-term to *medium or short term,* from *non-targeted* to *targeted,* and from *autonomous* to more and more *collaborative.*

These changes in dominant university research are legitimised by means of new insights concerning the nature of research. During the forties and fifties, the legitimisation of the expansion of the public financing of the university was based on the linear innovation model referred to earlier. The universities, so was thought, turned out *useful knowledge*, based on *disinterested basic research*. Applied research, therefore, was considered extraneous to the university. Vannevar Bush, the main advocate of this perspective, even stated that applied research tended to push out basic research. From the seventies onwards this axiomatic dichotomy between *basic* versus *applied* research has been called into question and new models of knowledge and knowledge production have been developed, such as Gerald Holton and Gerhard Sonnert's notion of 'Jeffersonian Science,' Donald Stokes's model of 'Pasteur's Quadrant' and Michael Gibbons defense of Mode 2 research.[21]

Many have welcomed these changes within the university and some even claim that the university is in some sense, as it were, going back to its roots. Ben Martin argues that there always have been multiple types of universities that coexisted within the national systems. Others believe that these changes are threatening the university. The OECD, normally one of the more fierce defenders of the third economic mission, warns that the science system,

> is facing the challenge of reconciling its traditional functions of producing new knowledge through basic research and educating new generations of scientists and engineers with its newer role of collaborating with industry in the transfer of knowledge and technology.[22]

## 5. The Changing Nature of Research - Teaching Nexus of the University

The combination of research and teaching within the same institution and by the same group of faculty is the traditional hallmark of the von Humboldtian, or modern research-based university. This combination of research and teaching often profits the students. In a recent report to the Higher Education Funding Council for England (HEFCE) on the interactions between research, teaching, and other academic activities some benefits of the linkage of research to teaching are identified.[23] Some of these benefits are of a direct nature. The students become exposed to the cutting edge of development of the knowledge base of the subject being taught and the benefit resulting from having a successful researcher as your teacher. This provides the student with an efficient role model for adopting and developing the skills and attitudes needed to succeed in higher education and in a possible future career as a researcher or knowledge worker. Some benefits are of an indirect nature, coming from the fact that good research universities can attract high caliber teaching staff, and the indirect benefits to student learning from the use of shared facilities and of the enhancement of resources resulting from a good research record of the university.

One of the caveats is, of course, that the research university has to be committed to deliver the teaching. However, there is some evidence that research universities and researchers are shrinking away from their teaching mission. It is a fact that teaching can sometimes interfere negatively with the research productivity of faculty and hence of the research institutions. Research oriented faculty, a recent study revealed, are more likely to view their research commitment as being competitive with teaching, and some aspects of the teaching negatively impact research.[24] Although most faculty continue to positively value the classic connection between research and teaching, staff and institutions,

> are almost invariably keen to engage in research - because it provides strong esteem drivers and is perceived to bring broadly based institutional and individual benefits - and this desire is reinforced by external assessment and public funding approaches.[25]

Research brings in respect and money, and with this money a certain autonomy can be bought, enabling the research universities to even better their research track record.

There is evidence that these trends are fundamentally altering the university landscape whereby the top of the research universities are out-competing the bulk of the rest of the universities. Top universities have adapted themselves better to the new economic rationale for the university and to the new funding schemes that have been set up to steer this process, than most other, often newer, universities.

Geuna identifies three groups of universities.[26] The top-level universities have adapted themselves well to the new situation. The less research-productive universities become more and more marginalised within the ever increasing competitive academic environment. These universities are forced to focus themselves on technological research or on teaching. In order to survive, these universities have to make do with whatever financing they can get. And this will become increasingly difficult, since money comes with research, and only secondly from teaching. The relevance of these bottom-level universities will become local. The biggest group of universities are situated between the top and the bottom. They, however, will have to choose: either adapt to the new model of knowledge production, and hence to the new economic rationale of the university, or become a teaching institution.

It could very well be the case that in the future the academic landscape will become more and more polarised: on the one hand we have the successful and rich research universities, on the other hand the teaching universities. Lacking in sufficient research and confronted with the massification of higher education, these teaching institutions will have to sell their teaching capacities in order to earn money.

This scenario is already partly visible in the trends of reform in higher education in European countries up to the start of the Bologna Process (1980-1998).[27] The main focus of the changes during this period was on reforms in institutional management, changing the existing relationship between the State and the higher education institutions by generating an increase in autonomy granted to higher education institutions - especially in the case of universities - and reinforcing the links of the higher education sector with the economic environment. Educational provisions became prone to higher levels of assessment and quality control. The assessment of higher education teaching and regulations concerning teaching qualifications, however, initially attracted less legislative attention.

The regimes for financing higher education institution were also influenced by the new legislation and affect deeply the educational mission of the institutions. Lump sum or block grant budgets for recurrent funding replaced earlier more earmarked funding strategies. However, course planning and restructuring became central because funding became increasingly based on objective funding formulae in which the number of students in specific types of courses played a decisive role, thereby encouraging higher education institutions to offer courses in priority subject areas, develop shorter and/or modular courses and take measures to promote access and reduce wastage. Greater institutional autonomy leads to linking the course offer more closely to the economic and social environment and in particular the labour market. As a result, the importance of contract-based funding increased and institutions attract additional money by selling their teaching and research services, either to the central or regional government or to bid for contracts on the open market with private organisations.

Another very important change during this period is the separation of basic research funding from teaching related funding, allowing the introduction of different allocation criteria for both. Funding of basic research becomes more and more modelled on the funding procedures organising the second and third stream research funding, that is, competitive and output-based research funding.

## 6. From 'Education' to 'Educability'

The pressures put on the modern university seem to endanger the traditional Humboldtian synthesis of research and teaching in the university. Universities that focus on research have to adapt to the changing financing structures by boosting up their research efforts, which often means tailoring down their teaching mission. Universities that perform badly on the research aspect get pushed even further down the road because of the well known Mattheus effect that is associated with the new research and output based financing structures for higher education. According to some, this has led to a crisis and even to 'the end of the university as we (have) know(n) it.'

Perhaps the idea of a university as exemplified by the Humboldtian university is itself an anomaly and a gross oversimplification of the real, complex and ever evolving field of different types of academic institutions, all labelled as universities. Perhaps, and even probably, there have always been different types of universities from the moment in history these institutions proliferated. This is the reason why Martin prefers to speak about the university species.[28] If this is indeed the case - and Martin develops some good arguments in favour of his position - then it would be too simple to speak of the end of the university. We would be lamenting the disappearance of a kind of institution that actually never existed, except perhaps as a idea and ideal.

However, the loosening of the ties between the research and the teaching mission of the university, as a result of the new economic rationale for the university of contributing to innovation and the information society, could very well threaten something more fundamental than the mere disappearance of an idea. Even the new roles of the university within the knowledge economy, information society and innovation system for which the new rationale was developed in the first place could be counteracted by the effects of the strained relations between research and teaching.

In a recent report on "Higher Education and Research for the ERA: Current trends and challenges for the near future" a STRATA-ETAN European Expert Group on foresight for the development of higher education/research relations stated that two of the main features of the knowledge society are the exponential rate with which knowledge accumulates, and the ever more rapidly changing technologies and work environments. Within the knowledge economy, the nature and organisation of labour is getting more and more complex. In such a context, so the expert group affirms, workers need to have learned to learn. They call this the notion of 'educability.' Furthermore, the knowledge workers must have the capacity to adapt but also be creative in rapidly changing working environments. This they call 'employability,' or, even better, 'sustainable employability.'[29]

Although this newspeak may to some signal the demise of a commitment to the more traditional goal of education to become enlightened citizens and competent professionals as exemplified by the Humboldtian programme, the expert group strongly underscores its opinion that the core competencies that appear central to this new concept of employability, like critical thinking, analysing, arguing, independent working, learning to learn, problem solving and decision making "quite clearly" benefit from the "old Humboldtian emphasis on the virtues of research-teaching cross-fertilisation." Because, as it turns out, the list of 'employability' competencies overlaps largely with the competencies involved in the exercise of the modern research activity. The 'traditional' model, therefore, "remains surprisingly relevant in the current context."[30]

One of the challenges the expert group signals for the higher education in this respect is providing for research-based teaching and active researchers as teachers not only on the graduate level but on the undergraduate level as well. However, if our review of the recent trends and developments within higher education, is correct, the rift could even become more profound, not only between undergraduate and graduate levels within a single university, but between universities as well.

Curiously, this line of questioning is largely absent from the debate initiated only this year by the European Commission on 'the role of the universities in the Europe of knowledge.'

## Notes

[1] European Commission, Green Paper on Innovation, COM (95) 688, 1995, 13.

[2] According to some, like, e.g., The European Association for International Education (EAIE), this leads to overstressing the servicing role of education and training in relation to employment and the economy.

[3] European Council, Presidency Conclusions: Lisbon European Council, 23 and 24 March 2000, 2000.

[4] Henry Etzkowitz and Loet Leydesdorff, "The Dynamics of Innovation: From National Systems and 'Mode 2' to a Triple Helix' of University-Industry-Government Relations," Research Policy 29 (2000): 109-123.

[5] In 1998 Edwin Manfield published an update of his 1990 documenting an increase of the relative share of processes and products based academic research, and a shortening of the time interval between the first commercial introduction of a new product or process based on a recent academic finding and the finding itself. Edwin Mansfield, "Academic Research and Industrial innovation," Research Policy 20 (1991): 1-12; Edwin Mansfield, "Academic Research and Industrial Innovation: An Update of Empirical Findings," Research Policy 26 (1998): 773-776. See, e.g., the work of McMillan, Narin and Deeds for research on the links between public science and innovation (G. Steven McMillan, Francis Narin and David L. Deeds, "An Analysis of the Critical Role of Public Science in Innovation: The Case of Biotechnology," Higher Education 29 (2000): 1-8). On collaborative research see, e.g., Evan M. Berman, "The Economic Impact of Industry-Funded R&D," Research Policy 19 (1990):

349-355; Paul David et al., "Is Public R&D a Complement or a Substitute fro Private R&D? A Review of the Economic Evidence," SIEPR Policy Paper No. 99-1 (1999); Paul David and Bronwyn H. Hall, "Heart of Darkness: Modeling Public-Private Funding Interactions inside the R&D Black Box," Research Policy 29 (2000): 1165-1183.

[6] See, e.g. Mowery and Rosenberg's Coupling theory and the Chain-Link model developed by Kline & Rosenberg.

[7] OECD, The Knowledge Based Economy (Paris: OECD, 1996), 15-16.

[8] Ammon J. Salter and Ben R. Martin, "The Economic Benefits of Publicly Funded Basic Research: A Critical Review," Research Policy 30 (3) (2001): 509-532.

[9] Pavitt, cited in Erik Arnold, et al., Research 2000 or Research 1950? Forskning 2000 and the Future of State Research Funding in Sweden (Brighton: Technopolis, 1999).

[10] Richard Florida "The Role of the University: Leveraging Talent, Not Technology," in Science and Technology Yearbook 2000, eds. Albert H. Teich et al. (Washington, DC: AAAS, 2000), 363-373.

[11] OECD, The Knowledge-Based Economy (Paris: OECD, 1996), 14.

[12] Etzkowitz and Leydesdorff, 115.

[13] OECD, The Management of Science Systems (Paris: OECD, 1999).

[14] Senker, Jacqueline et al. European Comparison of Public Research Systems, 1999, 12.

[15] EURYDICE, Two Decades of Reform in Higher Education in Europe: 1980 onwards (Brussels: EURYDICE European Unit, 2000).

[16] See, e.g., Geuna et al., Resource Allocation and Resource Performance: Final Report (Brighton: SPRU, 1999); Hugh Dickson, Resource Allocation in Universities: A Guide to Some Alternative Methods (London: The Commonwealth Higher Education Management Service, 1999).

[17] Jane Millar and Jacqueline Senker, International Approaches to Research Policy and Funding: University Research Policy in Different National Contexts. Final Report. Prepared for the Higher Education Funding Council for England (HEFCE) (Brighton: SPRU, 2000).

[18] Aldo Geuna, "The Changing Rationale for European University Research Funding: Are There Negative Unintended Consequences?" SPRU Electronic Working Papers Series, 1999, 12.

[19] Aldo Geuna, The Economics of Knowledge Production: Funding and Structure of University Research (Cheltenham: Edward Elgar Publishing, 1999), 22.

[20] Salter and Martin, 1999, 30.

[21] Gerhard Sonnert and Gerald Holton, Ivory Bridges: Connecting Science and Society (Cambridge, MA: MIT Press, 2002); Donald Stokes, Pasteur's Quadrant: Basic Science and Technological Innovation (Washington, DC: Brookings Institution, 1997); Michael Gibbons et al., The New Production of Knowledge: Science and Research in Contemporary Societies (London: SAGE Publications, 1994).

[22] OECD, The Knowledge-Based Economy (Paris: OECD, 1996), 7.

[23] J M Consulting Ltd and Associates, Interactions Between Research, Teaching, and other Academic Activities. Final Report to the Higher Education Funding Council for England as part of the Fundamental Review of Research Policy and Funding (London, 2000).

[24] Esther E. Gottlieb and Bruce Keith, "The academic research-teaching nexus in eight advanced-industrialized countries," Higher Education 34(1997): 397-419.

[25] J M Consulting Ltd and Associates, 1.

[26] Aldo Geuna, The Economics of Knowledge Production: Funding and the Structure of University Research (Cheltenham: Edward Elgar Publishing, 1999), 53.

[27] EURYDICE, Two Decades of Reform in Higher Education in Europe: 1980 onwards. (Brussels: EURYDICE European Unit, 2000). The definition of Higher Education includes both University and Non-University higher education institutions.

[28] Ben R. Martin, "The Changing Social Contract for Science and the Evolution of the University," in: Science and Innovation: Rethinking the Rationales for Funding and Governance, ed. Aldo Geuna et al. (Cheltenham: Edward Elgar, 2003), 7-29.

[29] STRATA-ETAN Expert Group, Higher Education and Research for the ERA: Current Trends and Challenges for the Near Future (Brussels: European Commission, 2002), 10.

[30] Ibid, 40.

# Bibliography

Arnold, Erik, Catherine Whitelegg and Ben Thuriaux. *Research 2000 or Research 1950? Forskning 2000 and the Future of State Research Funding in Sweden*. Brighton: Technopolis, 1999.

Bangemann, Martin. *Recommendations to the European Council: Europe and the Global Information Society*. European Council: Brussels, 1994.

Berman, Evan M. "The Economic Impact of Industry-Funded R&D." *Research Policy* 19 (1990): 349-355.

David, Paul, Bronwyn H. Hall and Andrew A. Tool. "Is Public R&D a Complement or Substitute for Private R&D? A Review of the Economic Evidence." SIEPR Policy Paper No.99-1, 1999.

David, Paul and Bronwyn H. Hall. "Heart of Darkness: Modeling Public-Private Funding Interactions Inside the R&D Black Box." *Research Policy* 29 (2000): 1165-1183.

Dickson, Hugh. *Resource Allocation in Universities: A Guide to Some Alternative Methods*. London: The Commonwealth Higher Education Management Service, 1999.

Etzkowitz, Henry and Loet Leydesdorff. "The Dynamics of Innovation: From National Systems and 'Mode 2' to a Triple Helix of University-Industry-Government Relations." *Research Policy* 29 (2000): 109-123.

European Commission. *Completing the Internal Market: White paper from the Commission to the European Council*, 1985.

European Commission. *The Single European Act*, 1986.

European Commission. *White Paper: Growth, Competitiveness, Employment. The Challenges and Ways Forward into the 21$^{st}$ Century*, 1993.

European Commission. *Europe's Way to the Information Society - An Action Plan*, 1994.

European Commission. *White Paper on Education and Training*, 1995.

European Commission. *Green Paper on Innovation*, 1995.

European Commission. *The Information Society: From Corfu to Dublin: New Priorities To Be Taken Into Account*, 1996.

European Council. *Presidency Conclusions: Lisbon European Council, 23 and 24 March 2000*. 2000.

EURYDICE, the Information Network on Education in Europe. *Two Decades of Reform in Higher Education in Europe: 1980 onwards*. Brussels: EURYDICE European Unit, 2000.

Florida, Richard. "The Role of the University: Leveraging Talent, Not Technology." In *AAAS Science and Technology Policy Yearbook*

*2000,* edited by Albert H. Teich, Stephen D. Nelson, Ceilia McEnaney and Stephen J. Lita, 363-373. Washington, DC: American Association for the Advancement of Science, 2000.

Geuna, Aldo. "The Changing Rationale for European University Research Funding: Are there Negative Unintended Consequences?" SPRU Electronic Working Papers Series, 1999.

Geuna, Aldo. *The Economics of Knowledge Production: Funding and the Structure of University Research.* Cheltenham: Edward Elgar Publishing, 1999.

Geuna, Aldo, Dudi Hidayat and Ben R. Martin. *Resource Allocation and Resource Performance: Final Report.* A study carried out for the Higher Education Funding Council of England. Brighton: SPRU, 1999.

Gibbons, M., C. Limoges, H. Nowotny, S. Schwartzman, P. Scott and M. Trow. *The New Production of Knowledge: Science and Research in Contemporary Societies.* London: SAGE Publications, 1994.

Gottlieb, Esther E. and Bruce Keith. "The academic research-teaching nexus in eight advanced-industrialized countries." *Higher Education* 34 (1997): 397-419.

J M Consulting Ltd. and Associates. *Interactions Between Research, Teaching, and other Academic Activities. Final Report to the Higher Education Funding Council for England as part of the Fundamental Review of Research Policy and Funding.* London: 2000.

Mansfield, Edwin. "Academic Research and Industrial Innovation." *Research Policy* 20 (1991): 1-12.

Mansfield, Edwin. "Academic Research and Industrial Innovation: An Update of Empirical Findings." *Research Policy* 26 (1998): 773-776.

Martin, Ben R. "The Changing Social Contract for Science and the Evolution of the University." In: *Science and Innovation: Rethinking the Rationales for Funding and Governance*, edited by Aldo Geuna, Ammon J. Salter and W. Edward Steinmueller, 7-29. Cheltenham: Edward Elgar, 2003.

McMillan, G. Steven, Francis Narin and David L. Deeds. "An Analysis of the Critical Role of Public Science in Innovation: The Case of Biotechnology." *Higher Education* 29 (2000): 1-8.

Millar, Jane and Jacqueline Senker. *International Approaches to Research Policy and Funding: University Research Policy in Different National Contexts. Final Report.* Prepared for the Higher Education Funding Council for England (HEFCE). Brighton: SPRU, 2000.

OECD. *The Knowledge-Based Economy.* Paris: OECD, 1996.

OECD. *The Management of Science Systems.* Paris: OECD, 1999.

OECD. *Science, Technology and Industry Outlook 2000: Science and Innovation.* Paris: OECD, 2000.

Salter, Ammon J. and Ben R. Martin "The Economic Benefits of Publicly Funded Basis Research: A Critical Review." SPRU Electronic Working Paper Series, 1999.

Senker, Jacqueline, Katalin Balazs, T. Higgins, Philippe Laredo, Emilio Munoz, Maria-Jesus Santesmases, Juan Espinosa de los Monteros, Bianca Poti, Emmanualle Reale, M. di Marchi, Anna Maria Scarda, Ulf Sandström, Uwe Schimank, Markus Winnes, H. Skoie and Halla Thorsteinsdottir. *European Comparison of Public Research Systems*. Brussels: European Union, 1999.

Sonnert, Gerhard and Gerald Holton. *Ivory Bridges: Connecting Science and Society*. Cambridge, Ma.: MIT Press, 2002.

Stokes, Donald E. *Pasteur's Quadrant: Basic Science and Technological Innovation*. Washington, DC: Brookings Institution, 1997.

STRATA-ETAN Expert Group. *Higher Education and Research for the ERA: Current Trends and Challenges for the Near Future*. Brussels: European Commission, 2002.

# CHAPTER SIX

## Student Expectations: How Was It For You?

*Tony Tricker*

**Abstract**

Nowadays, the prevailing orthodoxy is to think of students in Higher Education as customers of a service. This is partly as a result of the funding arrangements in the UK where students -or their parents- contribute directly to the cost of their education, and partly because of the growth of consumerism in public services. As a result, the student experience has become an important dimension in the measurement of quality of education.

The first part of the chapter will illustrate the ways in which student expectations have changed over the last three decades and what the drivers for this change have been. The nature of student expectations and the form of appropriate university responses are clearly complex issues, touching on almost all aspects of higher education. There is considerable value in sharing experience, knowledge and reflections about these matters.

The chapter will conclude by demonstrating how a web based interactive version of a 'Service Template,' QUEST (Quality Evaluation by Student Template) can highlight aspects of the student experience to generate a better fit between what students expect in a course of study and what they receive.

**Key Words:** Higher Education; Service Template; Student Expectations.

**1.        Changing Student Expectations**

It is clear to all who work in Higher Education (HE) that student expectations have changed over the last three decades. These expectations are now of greater complexity and a different order than in the past. Universities now find themselves being pushed on the one hand to respond to mounting student expectations, while on the other there are fears that the fundamental purpose of HE could be distorted or even lost if institutions go too far in the direction of placing HE on a commercial footing.

It is interesting to reflect how student expectations have changed over the past thirty years. In the 1970s a student at university may have expected:

1)   A place of scholarly reflection and learning;
2)   To obtain a degree;
3)   Enhanced employment prospects;
4)   Support by government funding;

5) Teacher student relationship to be one sided;
6) Very few expectations of teaching quality;
7) No concept of expectations of other stakeholders.

The 1980s and 1990s were very much a period of change. There was the transformation of polytechnics to universities in 1992. This changed the face of HE; we now had a sector responding more to the needs of society, providing vocational courses and catering for a more diverse set of students. New generations of students were entering HE and had a new set of expectations. The introduction of tuition fees has lead to students acting more like customers. How many times have we heard students say "I expect value for money?" Today students are seen increasingly as customers of a service. The supplier-driven, take-it-or-leave-it model which most HE institutions have followed in the past has been replaced by a focus on the student as a customer of a service.

Student -and parent- expectations are now high and as Davies points out, these now include[1]:

1) Flexibility and choice in the delivery of education;
2) Access to cutting edge technology;
3) A two way communication process between themselves and the university;
4) Consultation about the learning experience;
5) Accurate information about their courses, assessment procedures, complaints process, etc;
6) Honesty with respect to whether their needs can be met or not.

To these we may wish to add:

7) Quality and professionalism in the provision of services;
8) Access to suitably qualified teachers and appropriate learning support;
9) Value of study to career prospects.

It is possible to sketch some of the broad parameters that have caused student expectations to change. They include the rise of the student as a customer, which has been fuelled by the view by government that they should shoulder an increasing share of the cost of HE. Anyone who has dealt with student complaints will be familiar with students pointing out that they or their parents have paid money for their education and expect high standards of service and quality in return – "Am I getting value for money?" Competition among universities for the best students has in some sense resulted in overselling of courses. This has raised the level of student expectations, in that we may oversell the positive points. For example, teaching related to world class research, or students as part of a cutting edge experience. If these are not met, dissatisfaction may occur. Many students now work part time while in HE and as a result want a flexible learning environment, for example, 24/7 access to services. Not last in a drive of change, has been the influence of external agencies such as the Quality Assurance Agency (QAA), with its emphasis on the quality of the student experience. With its rolling programme of subject reviews there has been a heavy emphasis on identifying and enhancing the student experience and whether or not institutions are meeting student expectations.

In the future, universities will have to face the challenge that as students come to pay more of their tuition costs, there will be a new set of student expectations driven directly by the students themselves. There will be pressure for universities to be more responsive to student needs. Will soaring student debt fuel student expectations? "Graduates now leave with an average debt of £10000; under new arrangements this could be as high as £21000."[2] Another challenge facing universities will be the need to pay more attention to the student experience because of the introduction of institutional audits by the QAA. The importance of these in measuring the student experience can be illustrated by the following quote.

> Students will be put at the centre stage to drive up standards. They will have a forum to tip off auditors about any short comings. They will complete satisfaction surveys.[3]

It is not surprising, with the greater role of the student in assessing the quality of their educational experience, that HE institutions are devoting much more time improving the student experience. In many cases this has been carried out by 'bridging the gap' between what students expect and experience. By controlling the student learning environment HE institutions have been successful in bringing student experiences and expectations more in line. This has been achieved in my institution by such things as:

1) Changing curriculum design to enhance employability;
2) More flexible provision;
3) Improvement in teaching quality;
4) Improved student support;
5) Greater transparency.

The recent annual *Unite Student Living Report* provides a valuable insight into the way students view their university with respect to expectations.[4] During the current debate about student funding, it is interesting to note that the survey found that 58% of students think that they receive good value for money from their course, while 10% feel their course to be poor value. As Figure 1 from the Unite report indicates, 84% of students say their course meets or exceeds their expectations but 14% feel they have fallen short of expectations. From the same report, an area of concern is that dissatisfaction with a course increases the further into the course a student progresses (Figure 2). For first year students this is 8% and rises to 21% in year three. It is important to remember that in order to improve the student experience, their expectations have to be taken into account. Clearly the results from the Unite survey indicate that universities are falling short of this as students progress through their courses.

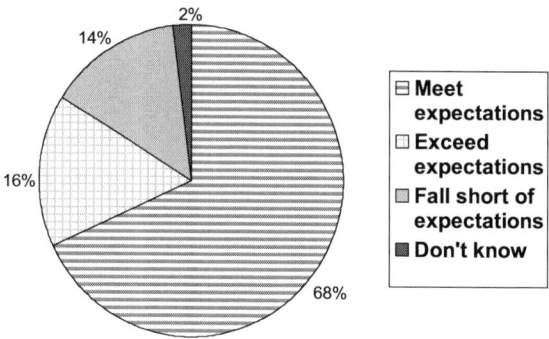

**Figure 1: Does your course meet expectations?**

| All students | 14% |
|---|---|
| Year of Study | |
| 1st Year | 8% |
| 2nd Year | 12% |
| 3rd Year | 21% |

**Figure 2: Fall short of expectations**

## 2. Management of Student Expectations

Universities need to take a more strategic approach to the management of student expectations. One possible solution is to outline the student experience more clearly or to be prepared to change student expectations. This is especially important in light of evidence which suggests that student expectations can be shaped significantly by a two way dialogue between "provider and customer."[5] As pointed out by Sander et al:

> HE has typically adopted an 'inside out' approach - with us on the inside assuming we know what students expect and want from HE. However, successful service industries have been shown to think 'outside in.' They research what customers expect of the service and then work to provide the service that meets those of customer expectations.[6]

It would seem sensible that an obvious step in the management of student expectations is to seek ways to understand these expectations that is adopt the 'outside in' approach suggested by Sander. Namely, in order to increase student satisfaction, we need to identify where gaps exist between the experience and expectations of students. Identifying where such gaps exist not only gauges the overall level of satisfaction, but reveals specific areas where improvements can be made to raise the level of student satisfaction and therefore the success of the service offered. The importance of closing the gap between what students expect and experience in order to improve the level of service was highlighted by Scott, "Good service provision does not necessarily mean doing everything the customer wants so much as bring the expectations of the service provider and customer closely together."[7] The next section outlines how the approach used by the service industry can be used to highlight where significant gaps exist between what students are expecting and what they are experiencing on a course.

## 3. The Template

Long et al. and Tricker et al. have adapted a tool used in the service industry, the Template, to measure the fit between customer expectation and experience, so that it would apply to the situation in which students, as customers, find themselves with their course provider, as service industry.[8,9] In the context of education courses, this translates as a gap that might exist between what students expect on their course and what they in fact experience. By using the Template we can be more proactive in closing the gap between what students, as consumers, expect and experience from their educator, the provider. Figure 3 illustrates this approach.

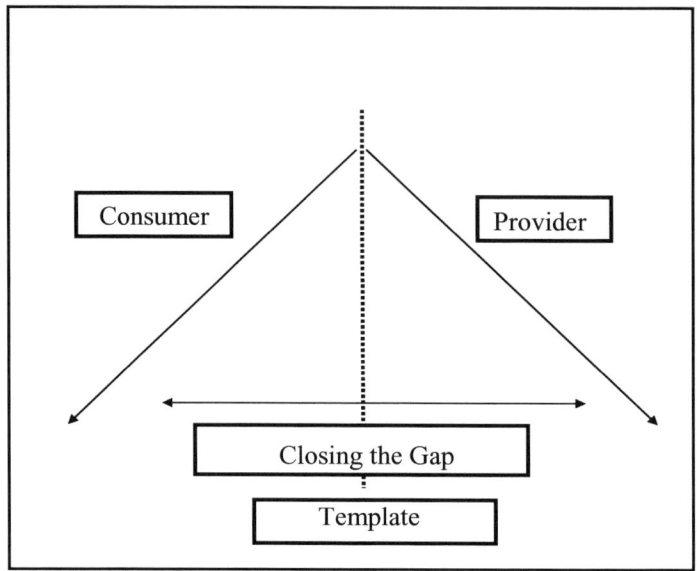

**Figure 3: Mind the Gap**

In brief, the Template adopts a radically different philosophy from the more conventional satisfaction survey. A number of aspects of interest are first identified. This is done by asking students what are the most important aspects of course provision to them. For each of these chosen aspects the Template offers a spectrum of possibilities, represented by distinct end-points on a scale, on which respondents locate a position corresponding to first what they expect in their course and second what they experience. The scale for a typical aspect is shown in Figure 4.

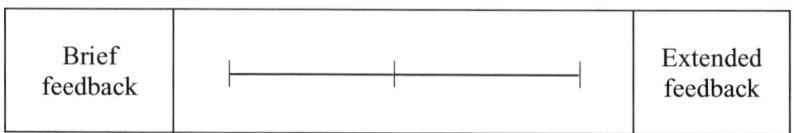

**Figure 4: Typical Template scale**

The aspects are identified by asking students to identify the most important aspects of course provision to them. A variety of methods are used to establish what the students themselves felt were the important aspects of course delivery, including focus groups and a paper based questionnaires.[10] Care is taken to ensure that the end-points are as far as possible value-free.

After the students have marked the two positions -one indicating what they *expect,* the other what they *experience-* the distance between the two -in other words the gap- is calculated for each of the aspects. The gaps identified by individual students are then combined with responses from other students at the same stage of the same course and analysed to produce comparative statistics. The most meaningful of these statistics is the so-called *satisfaction gap* associated with an aspect of course provision. This is the average across the student cohort of the absolute values of the difference between the two measurements. The absolute value is used to reflect that any difference between what is *expected* and what is *experienced* indicates dissatisfaction. The aspects included in the Template are then ranked in order of this satisfaction gap to establish the order of importance for taking action to close the gap.

Recently a web-based version of the Template, QUEST (QUality Evaluation Student Template), has been developed. A screenshot from QUEST is shown in figure 5. The students are asked for each aspect to position a slider on the continuum between two end points in order to indicate what they expect from their course. Once the process has been carried out for all aspects students are asked to repeat the process, but this time what they experience using the same endpoints. Hence the resulting *satisfaction gap* can be calculated.

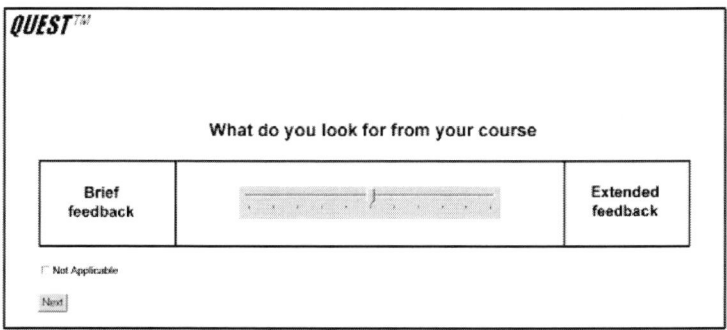

**Figure 5: Screenshot from QUEST**

4.      **Does the Template Work?**

To date the Template has been used to evaluate a number of postgraduate Distance Education course in several institutions and across a range of subject areas. The data has been collected from students at all stages of their course and whilst they are currently studying rather than on completion of units, so that their experiences are fresh. Informal feedback from students themselves suggests that they find the Template quick and easy to complete. Response rates have been reassuringly high.

There was also a need to examine the way in which the course teams used the information we provided about the gaps, or lack of them, that students identified between their expectation and experience of their course. Namely did course directors, given the information about their course from the Template, take appropriate action. After all, there would be no point using the Template, if the results could not be used to improve the quality of the courses.

The three course directors we used were responsible between them for three distance masters courses, Applied Statistics, Total Quality Management, and M.Ed. which were offered in Hong Kong, the UK, and Singapore respectively. It is fair to say that the directors expected the Template's findings to be mainly positive, in that they thought their publicity material, that is their course guides, handbooks, and induction procedures, would create not only a consistency of student expectations but also that students' expectations of their course would more or less match their experience of the course. The directors assumed that they had made it clear to students what the programme of study would be like so they were confident that there would be a close match of expectation to experience. If there were any problems it was thought these would cluster around the actual experience students had of their course.

It was accepted that there might be differences between the various years of a course. The idea of comparing student expectation with experience was itself a novel one to the directors, but in the main they did not think there would be much to question their faith in the quality of their courses, where 'quality' is defined as providing, within reasonable limits, what a student expects from their course. In other words, with a confidence based on 'standard' student evaluation procedures, they expected the gaps between student expectation and experience to be small, if they existed at all.

As directors expected, there were many areas where there was little or no gap between distance students' expectations and experience of their course.

The results from the Template showed the following aspects where students' experiences closely matched their expectations:

1) Course assessment to be by coursework, spread evenly over the life of the course, with clear assessment criteria and hand in dates, with the dissertation/long study to appear at the end of the course;
2) Personal feedback on their progress;
3) Detailed course information to be sent automatically;
4) Frequent residential study schools;
5) Course units to be interlinked.

Course directors found it comforting to know that, in these respects at least, no changes to the design of their course was necessary in order to meet their students' expectations. However, the Template results revealed a number of aspects with significant gaps, these being in the areas of feedback, tutorial support, assignment, and core text issues. The following two examples illustrate how the course director responded to evidence derived from the Template to close a gap between student expectation and experience on the course.

A. Core Text Issues

Students expected core texts for their course to be specified and that they should be provided as part of the service they pay for through their fee.

> Director's Response:
> *The current reading list only suggests texts and for many units no core text exists. I will need to alter the course handbook so as to specify core texts (where they exist) and also make it clear to the students that as post-graduates they will need to make use of a number of texts. I will also have to explain how much the fee would be increased by if we were to provide core texts as part of their course entitlement. This gap appears to have been created by a communication problem on my part.*

B. Assignment Issues

Students expected more assignments to be linked to their professional experience (that is, to be more applied than theoretical) and also expected more assignments to examine the application of theory to practice.

> Director's Response:
> *I feel very strongly that at master's level there has to be a core of theory that underpins the programme. This said, there are many assignments that do allow students to apply theory to practice, not least the dissertation which is intended to relate the course as a whole to their own professional experience. I need to manage student expectation better, especially during the induction sessions and in the course handbook.*

The course directors were able to recognise that their previous understanding of their course as derived from their experience and their existing 'standard' course evaluations had given them no understanding of the fit, or otherwise, between what students were looking for on a course and what they actually experienced, whereas the Template did provide this important information. The directors also recognised that the information about a possible gap at this point was critical to the success of their course, especially regarding retention, in that:

1) It is possible to identify the specific points where a student might be dissatisfied;
2) Once identified the student's experience can be managed in an appropriate way (for example, by changing relevant elements of the course);
3) Conversely, the student's expectation can be managed in an appropriate way (for example, the advertising material and induction programmes could be used to correct any misapprehensions students might have about what to look for on courses of this type so as to manage student expectation without changing the course itself);
4) If used over the lifetime of a course the director and course team would have a very clear idea as to the student experience and how it was changing so, again, the Template provides information that allows for the programme to be modified on the basis of firm data so as to enhance the quality of the student experience.

Thus the Template allowed for pinpoint accuracy in the identification and subsequent management of student expectation and experience, including areas where no action was either required or possible. It provided information that contradicted the directors' assumptions about their course, in that the directors had assumed that there would be little or no gap between what students expected and actually experienced on their course.

Another key finding from this study was that course directors need to be more aware of the need to manage student expectations effectively. It is easy to assume that a carefully written course guide will be equally carefully read by students, but this research indicates that such an assumption is not always well founded. Face-to-face induction sessions are necessary to reinforce the important messages that can be found in course guides. The Template identifies which of these are to be perceived as significant by students and so allows gaps to be closed before they widen into significant problems. At least for the courses under consideration in this article the Template indicated that there was no need to change elements of the programmes themselves, with all the cost and time implications of such alterations. Rather, student expectations needed to be better managed by means of improved communication. In this way the Template provides a much more efficient and targeted approach to the use of student evaluation.

## 5. Conclusion

In this chapter it has been shown how student expectations have constantly changed since the 1970s. The implication of this is that educational providers need to devote more attention to ascertaining just what the expectations and experiences of students are. By understanding these expectations they will be more successful in closing the gap between student expectation and experience. The Template has been shown to be successful in highlighting where these gaps are on a course. In doing so it has been found to be a valuable tool in 'bridging the gap' between what students expect and experience. The Template provided responses to two questions that should exercise the minds of all course providers 'How was it for you' and 'What should I do to make it better?'

## Notes

[1] Sarah Davies, "Marketing in Higher Education: Matching Promises and Reality to Expectations." In *Responding to Student Expectations*, 103-114 OECD, 2002.

[2] Colin Clarke, "A case for raising tuition fees." Times Higher Education Supplement, January 2003.

[3] Margaret Hodge, "Watch Dog Bitten." Times Higher Education Supplement, April 2002.

[4] Unite, *Students Living Report,* (2003).

[5] Richard James, "Students' Changing Expectations of Higher Education and the Consequences of Mismatches with the Reality." *Responding to Student Expectations*, 71-83 OECD, 2003.

[6] Paul Sander et al., "University Students' Expectations of Teaching." *Studies in Higher Education* 25 (1985): 309 - 324.

[7] Stephen Scott, "The Academic as Service Provider: is the customer always right?" *Journal of Higher Education Policy and Management* 21 (1999): 193-201.

[8] Peter Long et al., "Measuring the satisfaction gap: education in the market place." *Total Quality Management* 10 (1999): 172 – 778.

[9] Tony Tricker et al., "Evaluating Distance Education Courses: the student perception." *Assessment and Evaluation in Higher Education* 26 (1999):165-177.

[10] Margaret Rangecroft et al., "What is Important to Distance Education Students." *Open Learning* (1999):17 - 24.

## Bibliography

Baldwin, Gabrielle. "The Student as Customer." *Journal for Higher Education Management* 9 (1994): 131-139.

Booth, Anthony. "Listening to Students: Experiences and Expectations in the Transition to a History Degree." *Studies in Higher Education* 22 (1997): 205-219.

Harrison, Michael. "Service Quality in the Knowledge Age." *Measuring Business Excellence* 4 (2000): 21-26.

Scrabec, David. "A Quality Education is not Customer Driven." *Journal of Education for Business* 75 (2000): 298-300.

Shank, Michael. "Understanding Professional Service Expectations: Do we know what our students expect in quality education?" *Journal of Professional Service Marketing* 13 (2001): 10-20.

Staughton, Roy. "Towards a Simple, Visual Representation of Fit in Service Organisation: The Contribution of a Service Template." *International Journal of Operations and Production Management* 14 (1994): 76-85.

Swenson, Clive. "Customers and Markets: The Cus Words in Academe." *Change* 30 (1998): 10-15.

# CHAPTER SEVEN

# Let's Go Out and Learn

## *Paramita Atmodiwirjo and Yandi Andri Yatmo*

**Abstract**
    This chapter will discuss the place of learning, where learning happens, and the supportive role physical setting plays in the learning process. In particular it will examine the outdoor environment as a physical resource in architectural education, using a case study from the undergraduate design studio at the University of Indonesia. This studio makes use of learning in outdoor spaces as a part of the process in developing students' understanding of space. Through the process of *doing*, *observing*, and *making* in outdoor settings, the students come into direct interaction with the environment. They receive opportunities for direct experience of space and place, the sharpening and activation of body senses, and a new sensitivity towards the environment. The outdoor environment also gives opportunities for direct creation of space and place, and provides freedom from physical boundaries and built objects. The richness of environmental features supports the process and expands students' spatial vocabularies. In this program, learning activities in outdoor spaces have become a key element of the overall learning process alongside the learning activities in the *traditional design studio*.

Key words: outdoor; environment; learning; space; place; architecture; experience.

**1.    Introduction**
    In recent years, there has been an increased understanding of the important role of learning outside the classroom. The place for learning has been redefined in such a way that learning can take place anywhere beyond the *traditional classroom*. Learning outside the classroom has been a common practice in many educational institutions in various education levels. This practice includes learning through landscapes in natural outdoor space[1] as well as learning in the real situation with actual problems.[2] The learning process in these situations offers direct experience and interaction with the environment.
    This chapter will focus on a learning process in architecture that takes place within the context of outdoor, non-built space as the setting for learning. Architecture is a discipline that creates environment for people and has often been associated with physical buildings. However, architecture is also about space for human beings and their activities. "The

facades and the walls of the buildings are only the container, and the content is the internal space."[3] In the process we will describe here, we attempt to illustrate how the students' learning begins not with the examination of physically built objects or buildings, but with the experience of non-built spaces.

The discussion begins with a brief illustration of the role of natural environment in the process of architectural design. Then the use of outdoor environment as a learning resource is described through a case study in undergraduate architectural design studio at the University of Indonesia. In this case study, the role of outdoor environments in supporting the learning process is examined, as well as the benefits and the problems in its implementation. Finally, the chapter is summarised by addressing the issue of how this approach might contribute to the development of learning resource for higher education in general.

## 2. Role of Natural Environments in Architecture

The close relationship between architecture and environment is unquestionable. The understanding of the environment, whether natural or built, is an integral part in architectural design process. Learning architecture includes learning to create an object within a context. While the context might include physical environment as well as social environment, it is the natural physical environment that will become the focus of this discussion.

A piece of architecture is built on a piece of land, whether it is located in a rural environment or an urban environment. Understanding the place where it is to be built becomes an important part within the process of design as a whole. It provides an architect with the ideas that help him carry on with the process. Simonds described how the keen awareness of site can be a great significance in the planning process, and one of the architects that he interviewed explained how he attempted to know the site when starting a design work:

> ...I go each day to the piece of land on which it is to be constructed. Sometimes for long hours with a mat and tea. Sometimes in the quiet of the evening...sometimes in the busy part of the day...I go to the land, and stay, until I have come to know it. I learn to know its bad features...I learn to know its good features...and so I come to understand this bit of land, its moods, its limitations, its possibilities. Only now I can take my ink and brush and start to draw...[4]

The above passage, which we have very often quoted to our students when they worked in our design studio, indicates the richness that the environments possess, the richness that every architect needs to understand and explore. It illustrates the importance of developing awareness of the environment as a part of learning architecture. One cannot separate the architecture from its surroundings, as one cannot separate a human being from the environment where he lives.

What we attempt to achieve in the studio activities described below is developing the students' understanding of this close relationship between human beings and their environment. In doing so, we attempt to introduce the natural and unbuilt environment as a major element into the learning process.

## 3. Case Study: Undergraduate Design Studio Activities[5]
A. . Objectives and Approaches

The studio was the first design studio experienced by the students during their first year of studying architecture. The objectives were to develop students' understanding of architecture as space for human activities, and to raise the students' appreciation of architecture not as building shapes but as enclosures for human beings.

The objectives were set up in order to redirect the students' common predisposition to think that *architecture* was merely about *buildings*. We wanted the students to think about architecture as space as well as promote their appreciation of the unbuilt.

Several learning approaches were utilised in studio activities to achieve these objectives:

1) doing, simulating, and observing human actions and activities concretely,
2) experiencing and creating space and place directly, and
3) stimulating interaction and argumentation.

The students' learning process in this studio was mainly experiential, in which "...the knowledge is created through the transformation of experience".[6] In developing their understanding of architecture as human space, the students went through the four-stage cycle of experiential learning, illustrated in Figure 1and
Figure 2.[7]

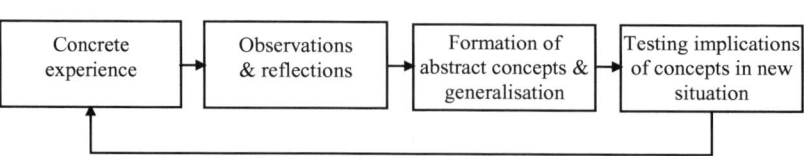

**Figure 1. Experiential learning cycle**

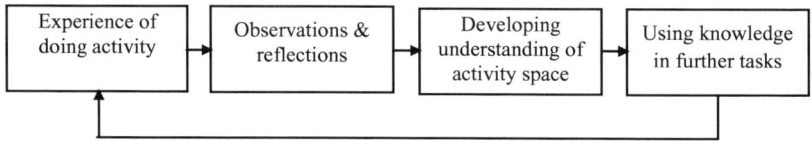

**Figure 2. Experiential learning in studio activities**

As illustrated in
Figure 2, at the beginning of the studio activities, the students were given a task in which they had to experience or interact with the environment. This was followed by an observation and reflection of what they were doing, in order to gain and develop an understanding of space for human activities. Their understanding then would be used in their further design exercises. Throughout the process, the outdoor environments gave a major contribution to the students' learning.

B. University Campus as Learning Sites

The majority of the studio activities were conducted in outdoor environments, using the university campus as sites of learning. Our university campus is located on the outskirts of the capital city of Jakarta. It occupies a site of approximately 318 hectares, most of which is undeveloped natural reservoirs and forest.

The campus offers rich natural environments with various opportunities. There are varieties of natural resources available, from the purposely designed landscape around the campus buildings, the open fields, the natural and built water features, to the natural forest. All are located within reach, and thus it becomes possible to utilise these resources as a part of learning activities on a regular basis. In addition, the local climate allows for year round outdoor learning.

C. Students' Learning: Doing, Observing and Making

During the learning process in this studio, the students were assigned a series of tasks, most of which were to be completed in groups. The tasks involved several activities in which they conducted direct interaction with the environment in *doing*, *observing*, and *making*.

*Doing*

In many of the tasks in this studio, the students began their interaction with the environments through *doing*. In some tasks, the students were assigned to go to a particular site and interact with the environment using their various senses. They watched places, objects, peoples, and what happened around. Sometimes we asked them to close their eyes and feel the environment with other senses; they heard and smelled their surroundings; they touched objects and materials. In addition to using their senses, the students were also asked to move in space. Movements are basic to the awareness of space, and movements also enable human being to have strong feeling for space and spatial qualities.[8] We introduced the students to various kinds of places, and let them experience being in free space, confined space, closed space, and open space. We let them learn the feeling of crowded, spacious, high, low, dark, bright, comfortable, uncomfortable, hot, cool, noisy, quiet, and other kinds of spatial experiences.

Other tasks were developed around everyday activities such as walking, sitting, or eating, in which the students simulated or acted these activities in outdoor environment.[9] In one of the tasks they were asked to experience walking. The activities were structured in such a way that the students experienced walking on various kinds of paths: flat, gently sloping and steep sloping. They explored which surfaces were easy and difficult to walk on. In another task they were asked to choose various kinds of places for sitting. For example, where they find comfortable to sit and where they can do different kinds of sitting. Finally, the students were asked to simulate the activity of eating together in groups, including choosing the location and conducting the activity.

All the above tasks were conducted in outdoor environments. The emphasis was on direct interaction with the environment, in which the students were expected to learn from what they did and what they experienced while interacting with the environment. We will now turn into the next aspect of the students' learning that makes their interaction with the environment more meaningful: *observing*.

*Observing*

An important part of the experiential learning cycle is the reflection of the students' experience. During and after the *doing* phase, the students were asked to observe and reflect on what they were experiencing. The students reflected on the two different experiences; the first was their experience of *the environment* and the second was the experience of *being in the environment*.

The outdoor environment offered a variety of environmental characteristics to explore. The students received a rich experience of various surfaces, textures, and natural boundaries or obstructions. This richness allowed the students to sharpen their senses toward inexhaustive characteristics of places: spacious, crowded, open, closed, cool, shaded, hot, quiet, noisy, etc. Many aspects of the environments have been experienced so often that we no longer notice their uniqueness; in essence, they become 'invisible.'[10] The tasks given to the students were aimed at activating and sharpening their body senses. "The development of sensory awareness helps one to 'see' more of the environment and it also helps one to see it in a way different from before."[11] This was a very important exercise in understanding space in architecture.

Alongside the understanding of the environment, the students also got a chance to observe *being in the environment*. This covers one of the key objectives of the studio: understanding architecture as human space. "With the positions and movements of our bodies we *arrange* space."[12] Figure 3 illustrates how the students developed their understanding of body position and movement in space through these activities. In this example of students' analysis, the student summarised the spatial aspects of walking and sitting, the various kinds of sitting and walking, as well as various kinds of environmental characteristics that can support sitting and walking.

 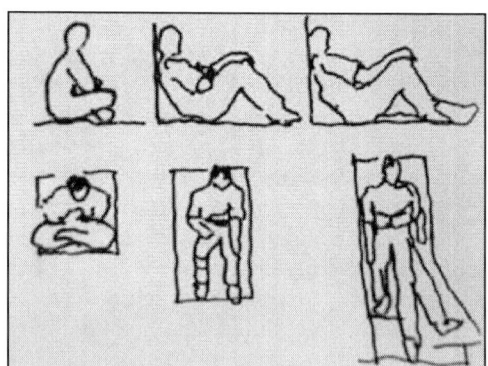

**Figure 3. Students' analysis of 'walking' and 'sitting'**

The students also analysed and developed their understanding of another important spatial aspect: the relationship between human beings in space.[13] They observed the body movements, positions, and relations in group activities where more than one person was involved. Based on this observation they were expected to develop their own understanding of space for human activities and the spatial characteristics required for those activities.

By doing and observing activities in outdoor, non-built spaces, the students were encouraged to free themselves from their previous knowledge of built and physical space. They formed their own understanding based on their direct experience. In the final task of eating together, the students were free to choose where and how they should eat, and to ignore the usual settings for meals. By ignoring the facts about the usual settings like the dining table or the restaurant, the students were encouraged to concentrate on the essence of the activity.

*Making*

The major thing about architectural design is "… to create something which other people will experience and which is in some way or other original and new."[14] The process of *making* becomes an integral part of the learning process in architectural education. "…without the experience of making the theoretical learning of a student remains static and not tested."[15] The part of *making* in this studio was done through the students' direct creation of space and place. After they developed their understanding of space based on their own experience and observation, they were asked to go further to the next stage of *making*, to implement their ideas of space. They conducted the act of building, which could be described as "…a cyclical process capable of connecting the realm of idea to its reality through the act of construction itself."[16]

The process of *making* began with the students developing their ideas of space for human activities. In one example of the studio exercises, we asked students to think about the space for a 'life-drawing' activity. They should think of all spatial requirements for that activity, and develop the ideas of space that could accommodate these requirements. Figure 4 show one of the students' work in this exercise. It shows that in developing this idea, this student took into account only the spatial characteristics that were essential for the activities, such as various positions of models, various eye height levels for drawing, direction of light and other environmental comfort. None of the physical objects such as chairs, lamps, and walls were seen in the students' spatial ideas. The students freed themselves from the physical boundaries of indoor space and from the common physical objects.

 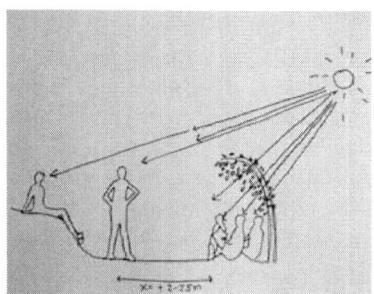

**Figure 4. Students' ideas of space for 'life drawing' activity**

In another task, the students were asked to create an exciting journey (*perjalanan yang menarik*). Their task was to create something that would enable people to experience a journey that was not boring or monotonous but full of joy and surprises. The students' process of planning and building the structures incorporated the various kinds of walking that they had explored previously. They combined various objects and materials together to create paths, boundaries, and obstructions, which defined a place for an exciting walking experience. After they completed the *making* process, they tested their creation by experiencing it and evaluated how it actually accommodated the feeling and experience that they would like to convey.

The process of *making* was completed entirely in outdoor space, which offered the opportunity to build 1:1 models and structures. Such things might be very difficult to build inside the classroom with limited space. The outdoor natural environment also offered a rich variety of materials for the students to use in building their structures. This richness of the environment also meant the possibilities for direct manipulation of the environment. The students could easily erect structures, dig holes, heap stones, pierce branches to the ground, or any other act of *making*.

The outdoor environment provided opportunities for the students for a direct creation of space and place. In addition, the emptiness of outdoor space provided freedom from the physical, built, tangible, and anything within the limits or boundaries. The students were encouraged to create something out of nothing, and thereby free their mind from what had been built. They were encouraged to be creative and to seek any possible alternatives in creating space and place. Another important aspect in the process of *making* was that the students did not only create their own objects but also learned to integrate their objects and structures into the existing environment, as well as to relate them with the spatial experiences of their body. This integration was an important part of learning how they could relate the body, space, and architecture with the surroundings.

Partly because the students were encouraged to make use of the available materials in their surroundings, and partly because the process included trial-and-error exploration, the physical outcomes of the *making* process seemed rough, unfinished, and far from perfect. The outcome did not represent the tidiness of material and construction that was usually found in the practice of architecture. However, the emphasis here was on the understanding of space and place, therefore the process was much more important than the final physical outcome.

D. Students' Appreciation of the Process

The success of the learning process does not depend on the method alone. Students play a major role within the process, especially in student-centred education where "... the content and knowledge occurs as a result of student learning, of the students constructing it for him or herself."[17] Thus, to enable students to gain the most from their learning, it is very important that students understand the objectives of the learning process.

Some of the feedback that we received from the students after they completed these tasks indicated that the objectives of the tasks were somewhat unclear. Although many of them enjoyed doing the activities in the outdoor space, some still found it difficult to understand the relationship between what they were doing and what they were actually learning. One drawback that we observed from this process was that the physical outcome that the students produced, as explained before, seemed rough and imperfect. As a result, some of the students questioned the value of the resulting physical structures which were ephemeral and thus were not perceived as *real architecture*. To overcome these problems, we needed to further explain the purpose of these activities. In future some adjustments to the structure of these tasks will need to be made so that the students will better appreciate the objectives of the activities.

**4.      Outdoor Learning: Opportunity in Architectural Education**

The case study presented here illustrates the opportunities that the outdoor place offers in supporting the learning process in architectural education. This setting supported the process of experiential learning and allowed direct experience in and with the environment.

Being in outdoor space encouraged the feeling of freedom for students. As a result, the studio was no longer defined by the classroom walls. Being in non-built spaces allowed the students freedom from physical boundaries and physical objects. The students learned to free their minds from anything physical, and concentrate on how they could create the place in a non-built space. It offered opportunity for the students to experience direct stimulus from an open, non-built space, the experience of *being there in space*.

The outdoor setting also offered a rich environment that supported the processes of *doing, observing,* and *making*. This allowed students to heighten their awareness of various environmental conditions. The various characteristics of outdoor natural spaces expanded students' spatial vocabularies: the concepts of boundaries, shelters, environmental comfort, spaciousness, and crowding. Such concepts could also be taught in theories, but were made more real through direct experience.

There are also more practical advantages to learning architecture in outdoor places. Besides the direct interaction with the materials and the environmental features, the possibility for easy manipulation of the environment and the creation of physical structures is less limited in outdoor environments than it is within classroom walls.

This case study illustrated how the outdoor environment offers various opportunities to support learning, however we do not intend to argue that learning in outdoor space is better than learning in traditional classroom. Rather, we believe that learning activities in outdoor space support and enhance learning activities in the traditional design studio.

> It seems obvious that more than a single approach to teaching-learning is necessary... how to integrate experiences from the field, the classroom, and the library... perhaps this integration is the essential element if the field learning is to be more than just a social outing from the school building.[18]

The description of the case study above makes it clear that the role of outdoor space in our studio is more than just an outdoor location for learning. Indeed we attempt to exploit its potential to support the students' learning in understanding space. This case study illustrates the possibility of using the outdoor learning environment as an alternative learning resource.

However, we realise that this case study cannot be easily generalised. For example, the case study described above requires a temperate climate which allows for outdoor learning on a regular basis. While the majority of institutions in tropical climates would be able to conduct this type of activity easily, it would be more difficult in harsher climates. Also, while there are a few institutions which have huge amounts of outdoor resources on the doorstep, many others have their campus buildings in dense urban areas and therefore have limited access to the outdoor natural environment.

Finally, the case study is limited to the learning process in architecture, and it is not our intention to generalise how it could be applicable to other subjects. The requirements of each subject vary, and the role and the importance of outdoor environment also differ from one discipline to another. Nevertheless, our discussion suggests a possible way of using physical learning settings, and illustrates the relationship between the human being and environment and how this relationship can become an integral part of the learning process.

# Notes

[1] Wendy Titman, Special Places, Special People: The Hidden Curriculum of School Grounds (Surrey: WWF UK/Learning through Landscapes, 1994), 65-75.

[2] Robert Sommer & Franklin Becker, "Learning outside the Classroom," in Learning Environments, eds. Thomas G. David and Benjamin D. Wright (Chicago: The University of Chicago Press, 1975), 75-81.

[3] Bruno Zevi, Architecture as Space: How to Look at Architecture (New York: Horizon Press, 1974), 24.

[4] John O. Simonds, Landscape Architecture: The Shaping of Man's Natural Environment (London: Iliffe Books, 1961), 48.

[5] This case study mainly presented the learning process developed by Siti Utamini in Architectural Design Studio 1 at the Department of Architecture, University of Indonesia, where the authors have joined her teaching team. The author would like to thank for her permission to use the documentation of the students' works. The students' analyses were redrawn from the original.

[6] David A. Kolb, Experiential learning: Experience as The Source of Learning and Development (Englewood Cliffs, NJ: Prentice Hall, 1984), 38.

[7] Kolb, 21.

[8] Yi-Fu Tuan, Space and Place: The Perspective of Experience (London: Edward Arnold, 1977), 12.

[9] Yandi Andri Yatmo and Paramita Atmodiwirjo, Learning through Everyday Experience. [on-line] (ADC-LTSN, 2001, accessed 1 June 2003); available from http://www.lancs.ac.uk/palatine/s-v-presentations/yatmopaper.doc

[10] Thomas G. David, "Environmental Literacy," in Learning Environments, eds. Thomas G. David and Benjamin D. Wright (Chicago: The University of Chicago Press, 1975), 169.

[11] Ibid, 163-164.

[12] Karen A. Franck and R. Bianca Lepori, Architecture Inside Out (West Sussex: Wiley-Academy, 2000), 37.

[13] Tuan, 34.

[14] Bryan Lawson, How Designers Think: The Design Process Demystified (Oxford: Architectural Press, 1997).

[15] Walter Gropius, Proceedings (ASCA Press, 1959), 59, as quoted in William J. Carpenter, Learning by Building: Design and Construction in Architectural Education (New York: Van Nostrad Reinhold, 1997), 17.

[16] Carpenter, 2.

[17] Greg Light and Roy Cox, Learning and Teaching in Higher Education: The Reflective Professional (London: Paul Chapman, 2001), 33.

[18] Sommer and Becker, 80-81.

## Bibliography

Andri Yatmo, Yandi and Paramita Atmodiwirjo. *Learning through Everyday Experience.* ADC-LTSN 2001. <http://www.lancs.ac.uk/palatine/s-v-presentations/yatmopaper.doc> (1 June 2003).

Carpenter, William J. *Learning by Building: Design and Construction in Architectural Education.* New York: Van Nostrad Reinhold, 1997.

David, Thomas G. "Environmental Literacy." In *Learning Environments*, edited by Thomas G. David and Benjamin D. Wright, 161-179. Chicago: The University of Chicago Press, 1975.

Franck, Karen A., and R. Bianca Lepori. *Architecture Inside Out.* West Sussex: Wiley-Academy, 2000.

Gropius, Walter. *Proceedings*, 59. ASCA Press, 1959. Quoted in William J. Carpenter, *Learning by Building: Design and Construction in Architectural Education* (New York: Van Nostrad Reinhold, 1997), 17.

Kolb, D. *Experiential Learning.* Englewood Cliffs, NJ: Prentice Hall, 1984.

Lawson, Bryan. *How Designers Think: The Design Process Demystified.* Oxford: Architectural Press, 1997.

Light, Greg and Roy Cox. *Learning & Teaching in Higher Education: The reflective professional.* London: Paul Chapman, 2001.

Simonds, John O. *Landscape Architecture: The Shaping of Man's Natural Environment.* London: Iliffe Books, 1961.

Sommer, Robert and Franklin Becker. "Learning Outside the Classroom." In *Learning Environments*, edited by Thomas G. David and Benjamin D. Wright, 161-179. Chicago: The University of Chicago Press, 1975.

Titman, Wendy. *Special Places, Special People: The Hidden Curriculum of School Grounds*. Surrey: WWF UK/Learning through Landscapes, 1994.

Tuan, Yi-Fu. *Space and Place: The Perspective of Experience*. London: Edward Arnold, 1977.

Zevi, Bruno. *Architecture as Space: How to Look at Architecture*. New York: Horizon Press, 1974.

# CHAPTER EIGHT

# The Hidden Presumptions of Commercially Derived Quality Management in Higher Education

## *Trudi Cooper*

**Abstract**
  Adoption of commercially derived quality management techniques in higher education worldwide has led to changes in the language used to describe both purposes of higher education and relationships between teachers and learners within higher education. This chapter examines whether the presumption that business relationships can be applied to the context of higher education can be justified. Commercially derived methods of quality management rely upon tacit assumptions that there are 'businesses,' with 'customers' who buy 'products.' If these terms cannot be meaningfully applied to education, then commercial methods of managing and measuring quality are not applicable to universities.
  The chapter reports part of a study of quality management in higher education in Australia. The study concludes that the current usage of the term 'quality' in Australian higher education relies heavily on the presumption that the language of business is applicable to education, but examination of key documents illustrates that application of business language to universities uncovers irresolvable contradictions. The findings of this study suggest that quality in higher education must be re-conceptualised to take account of differences between the context of education (its purposes, the nature of its internal and external relationships) and that of business.


## 1. Introduction

  Quality management has become a political concern in all Organization for Economic Co-operation and Development (OECD) countries as higher education systems have expanded to provide education to a greater proportion of the post secondary population.[1,2] The most widespread response to this concern has been to apply commercially derived quality management methods to universities.[3,4] This begs questions about whether the purposes, roles and relationships tacitly assumed within quality management models can be found within higher education. This question has a broader significance because quality management methods have been applied to many types of non-commercial enterprise. It has been argued elsewhere that the application of commercially derived management methods forces universities to distort their own understanding of their purposes, roles and relationships in order to fit with the implicit assumptions of commercial quality management models.[5]

This chapter reports an Australian study of quality management in higher education that illustrates tensions arising from a poor fit firstly between the assumptions of quality management and the purposes, roles and relationships within higher education, and secondly between students as customers of higher education and the Australian government's intended purposes of higher education, which are in some iterations more limited and narrowly focused than many conventional conceptions. Attempts at resolving the mismatch between higher education and the concept of customers by applying the concept of 'stakeholder' moves the locus of the problem, creating irresolvable problems with the use of many of the commercially derived quality management methods.

## 2. Background

The Australian context for higher education is different from the British context in two key ways. Firstly, Australian universities are 'young' in world terms. Secondly Australian universities developed in a colonial context. The oldest universities in Australia were modelled on the English concept of university, but the colonial context meant that Australian universities were less central to social and political culture within Australia than their English counterparts. Whilst in the 19$^{th}$ century British universities, especially Oxford, trained politicians for Westminster, Bishops for a global church, and administrators for a global empire, Australian universities did not have that role. Instead, Australia was on the receiving end of the British university cultural exports, as an administered colony. The effects of this colonial heritage remain today. Of the post-war Australian prime ministers, three attended Oxford University (Gorton, Frazer, Hawke), three attended Sydney University (McMahan, Whitlam, Howard), two attended Melbourne University (Menzies and Holt), one attended the University of Western Australia (Hawke), and three were not university educated (Chifley, McEwen, and Keating).[6] The effects of the 'cultural cringe' on higher education (where the cultural products of the England are assumed to be of more value than those locally produced) affected Australian universities until recent times. Even into the last decade of the 20th century Australian universities annually recruited large numbers of overseas staff to fill university teaching and research positions. The effects of this are evidenced by research showing Australian university staff are much more likely than their British colleagues, to have gained at least one of their degree level qualifications overseas.[7]

Key milestones in the post-war history of the Australian university have included the social justice agenda of the Whitlam government in the 1970s, which enacted the bill abolishing of student fees at universities and extended the Federal government role in higher education,[8] and the 'clever country' policies of the Hawke government in the 1980s that marked the beginning of government policy to use higher education as a driver of economic growth.[9] The purpose of this policy was to transform the Australian economy from its high dependence on 'primary' production in agriculture and mining with relatively undeveloped manufacturing and service sectors, to a less vulnerable economic base through a higher contribution from tertiary services industries in the 'knowledge economy.' This economic strategy required more of the population to be educated to a higher level. As Marginson and Considine note, the other -and possibly main- political purpose served by the expansion of higher education in the 1980s was that it absorbed excess youth unemployment.[10] However, neither Labor nor Coalition governments have been willing to foot the bill for this expansion as the per capita figures for university spending illustrate.[11,12] The recent phase of university reform began in 1987. This led to the amalgamation of colleges and institutes of technology with universities that: ended the binary higher education system; began the massification of higher education; and marked the start of a progressive shift in the burden of cost away from Federal government and towards the student.[13] The figures show that this latter process has accelerated since 1996, as the Howard Coalition government has intensified its program of introducing (pseudo) markets into public services and pursuing policies to extend the privatisation of higher education.[14] The current political context of higher education policy in Australia, as in many other countries, is one where market ideology is being applied to non-commercial enterprises (government, education, health, welfare) in an ideologically driven attempt to commodify human interactions that had previously been judged according to different standards.[15]

Quality management is a condition of Federal government funding.[16] Current processes require universities to individually collect data to prove that they are meeting their self-determined goals and to establish processes to ensure "continuous quality improvement."[17] These quality processes are externally audited once every five years by the Australian Universities Quality Agency (AUQA), a quasi-independent body receiving government funding to perform this task.[18]

**3.     Purposes in Higher Education in Australia**

English models of university education through colonisation have provided the strongest influences shaping the idea of university in Australia. Since the 1990s, Australian universities have been influenced by the 'globalised' market for education.[19] To understand how the idea of purpose has been shaped in Australian universities it is necessary to look both at Australian university history and also the development of the idea of university in England and other English-speaking countries including North America. Histories of individual universities and of university systems in many countries show that there is no single concept of university; it is variable between institutions and that it is variable within a single institution over time.[20,21] Commentaries on the histories of universities have been provided extensively elsewhere and what follows is a distillation of some of the main purposes. The literature generates a number of themes.

Many ideas have influenced modern conceptions of university. David Preston suggests that in the 'modern' era, post 1945, ideas that have been influential in previous historical periods may co-exist with current trends, but that they are interpreted through the dominant societal values of managerialism, consumerism, commercial, and economic utility and the primacy of scientific and technological knowledge, (although he suggests that universities do not necessarily reflect these values as much as might be expected).[22] His overview also illustrates that practical and vocational education has a history dating at least from mediaeval times, as does the contrary idea of separation of universities from the practical concerns of the world.

In the post 1947 period many changes have taken place in universities throughout the English-speaking world including extensive discussion about the changing role for universities. Within 'modern' post-1947 universities debate about purpose is still influenced by: liberal university movement;[23,24] ideas about student development creating a more tolerant society;[25] ideas that the university marked the civil society;[26] Greek and mediaeval concepts of the 'learned man;'[27] enlightenment ideas supporting humanism and rationality overcoming ignorance;[28] universities as training schools in law and theology and later medicine;[29,30] education for liberation and radical social change;[31] higher education as vocationalism;[32] higher education to obtain personal wisdom;[33] higher education for social transformation;[34] higher education as a driver of economic growth;[35] higher education for social well being;[36] higher education and the development of human capital;[37] and ideas of unity of research and teaching.[38]

The conflicting purposes of higher education can be categorised according to whether the intention is to provide individual benefit to students or broader societal benefit and according to whether 'benefit' is conceived normatively or transformatively. This provides the following typology outlined in Table 1.

**Table 1: Normative/transformative versus individual/societal orientations towards conceptualisations of university purpose**

| Transformative- individual | Transformative- social |
|---|---|
| Seek new knowledge for its own sake irrespective of considerations of immediate utility and profit; to question what others accept irrespective of social disapproval; personal wisdom; individual freedom from the restrictions imposed by conventional beliefs and expectations. | Emancipative and transformative social and personal change; social movements and political change through personal change; to increase individual tolerance of difference. |
| **Normative- individual** | **Normative- social** |
| Student development within normative bounds of culture 'the cultured man'; student development to meet the utilitarian aspirations of students for their future employment and personal life goals within the existing social order; | Normative professional and vocational preparation, to both serve industry (or empire) and the professions, including business, welfare and personal services in the existing social order |

There are dangers if these methods of categorisation are taken as definitive, as schema like this accentuate some oppositions and hide others.[39] Schema based upon alternative oppositional pairings will accentuate different features.[40]

## 4. Purposes, Roles and Relationships in Higher Education

Different purposes of education give rise to different roles and relationships both within and between academe and society. To illustrate the significance of this, Table 2 shows the implications of the conceptual archetypes identified in the schema for roles and relationships within university and between universities and society.

**Table 2: Four different orientations towards purposes in education and implications for roles and relationships**

|  | Normative Individual | Normative Societal | Transformative Individual | Transformative Societal |
|---|---|---|---|---|
| Pedagogic orientation | Student development | Assure minimum skill competence | Excellence in academic discipline | Consciousness raising, social activism, political change |
| Academic staff role | Teachers and mentors | Assessor of professional competence and work skills | Transmitting knowledge; producing new knowledge; | Partners in learning |
| Student staff relationship | Student as student | Student as trainee | Student as scholar; student as disciple | Student as learning partner, colleague |
| University Relationship with industry | University 'civilises' industry through educating its future leaders | University responsive to needs of professions and industry | Higher education ignores industry | HE transforms people who transform society including industry and commerce |

Many of the debates about what should be assessed in higher education can be explained by differences in pedagogic orientation arising from difference in perspective on the purpose of education. Many courses combine and balance multiple purposes in their curriculum and in learning experiences offered to students. The differences in conception of purpose give rise to very different assumptions about the nature of the student role, the nature of the academic role and the nature of the relationship between students and academic staff, see Table 2. Whilst a visit to any university would uncover a diversity of opinion on the relative primacy each purpose, it is clear that not all the roles and relationships are mutually compatible. This is a potential source of role strain,[41] and may partially explain the increases in work related stress reported in recent surveys of university staff.[42, 43]

## 5. Purpose, Roles and Relationships in Commercially Derived Quality Management Methods

According to Kim Cameron and Wesley Sine, in the literature on commercial quality management, quality is used in six distinct technical specialist ways, all of which differ from common usage. All forms of quality management rely on one or other of the technical meanings of quality and these are referenced to either attributes of the product or referenced to customer satisfaction or customer expectation of the product.[44] Quality management assumes there are products, (where the term product includes services) and assumes that there is a customer relationship between the business and the person who pays for the product. An important lesson from commerce that appears to be overlooked in quality assessment in higher education is that the different technical meanings of quality imply very different commercial goals and means of measurement. The different goals are not mutually compatible. For example, W Edwards Deming,[45] who supported cultural approaches to quality, argues strongly against numerical measurement of efficiency because it encourages localised optimisation to the detriment of the overall goals of the organisation. So what happens to the purposes of higher education if quality management methods, that assume a customer relationship, are applied to higher education? This is one of the questions posed in the research.

A. .Research Findings

The research project was concerned with a critical examination of the conceptual basis and practical application of quality management policy in Australian universities in the period since 1999. Three types of documentation pertaining to quality in Higher Education in Australia were examined. Firstly, Government policy on quality in Higher Education and its associated justificatory 'research' was examined. This established the dominant or hegemonic presentation of the ideology of quality management in Australian Universities. Secondly, the formal 'quality plans' for five universities in Western Australia, representative of a variety of types of university, as categorised by Andrews et al., were examined.[46] This established the public face of the response by university management to the government's higher education quality policy. Finally examples of the reports of AUQA quality review panels whose task it was to report on quality in clusters of programs were examined. The purpose of this was to find out how review panels reported the application of quality policy at the micro level within universities. The panel reports are not discussed in detail in this chapter.

## 6. Higher Education Policy and Quality

Although the study was primarily concerned with the post 1999 period, the quality policies developed during this time were a response to the perceived deficiencies of prior quality management. For this reason, this account briefly outlines conceptualisations of quality in higher education from 1987 onwards. Conceptualisation of quality in higher education between 1987 and the present day has not stayed constant. In the early period (1987-1993), quality was conceptualised in fairly conventional ways as standards within disciplines. [47,48,49,50] In the period 1993-1995 'whole of institution' quality assessment was tried.[51] By the end of this period the equation of quality with academic standards had been criticised on a number of grounds including, the difficulties in judging standards across disciplines; the problem of deciding equivalence of standards between disciplines; and the inward looking nature of assessment, especially where standards are determined wholly within academia.[52] In this period between 1996-1998, quality policy stalled.[53]

In the period 1998-2001, quality was conceptualised as fitness for purpose and customer satisfaction.[54] In line with the recommendations of the West report,[55] the student was considered as the primary customer of universities.[56,57] This was politically expedient because during this period the burden of cost was being rapidly transferred onto the student, and the idea of students as customers of universities fitted easily with the market philosophy that underpinned government policy, and might ultimately legitimate higher education being presented entirely as a private 'good' for the sole benefit of the student. The idea of students as customers also fitted easily with commercial quality management techniques, which universities were being encouraged to use.

The conceptualisation of the purpose of universities as the preservation, transmission and expansion of human knowledge was articulated in the 1998 West report, "Learning for Life," where the purpose of university education is also expressed as enabling students to achieve personal fulfilment and to contribute to "society, the workplace and the nation."[58] The purpose of the modern university is "to open minds, to strengthen and discipline cognitive powers and sensibilities of mind, to refine the mind, and to create effective and efficient learners and knowledge builders."[59] The focus in this rendition is both highly individual and normative. Societal goals are conceived as an indirect consequence of the achievement of normative- individual goals. In this period, students are assumed to be both the customers and the products of universities, see for example, the government 1999-2001 triennial report.[60] However, the idea of student as customer did not fit with some parts of government policy, especially those concerned with using universities as a means to achieve societal goals. This leads to a very narrow interpretation of the purpose of higher education.

The most recent review of higher education, "Higher Education at the Crossroads," initiated in 2002 and still continuing, reiterates the Government view that higher education should promote "the pursuit, preservation and transmission of knowledge" and values both 'curiosity driven' and 'use inspired' research to enable both personal intellectual development and autonomy and to provide skills formation and educational qualifications to prepare individuals for the workforce.[61] The document emphasises however that the government views the purpose of higher education as more than just preparing students for jobs stating that higher education should contribute to "the fulfilment of human and societal potential, the advancement of knowledge and social and economic progress." The statements in this report include both the normative-individual purposes identified in the West report, and other purposes. Statements about advancing knowledge and understanding may also be read in ways that imply transformative-individual purposes.

In the later period 2002 onwards, policy documents no longer refer explicitly to students as customers but refer instead to universities as having multiple stakeholders.[62][63] This appears to resolve some of the difficulties of lack of fit between the private relationship of student as customer and the government's desire for universities to deliver identifiable short-term societal benefits. Difficulties emerge however, because the quality management methods developed in commercial settings tacitly assume customer relationships and it is not clear that they can be applied in a stakeholder context.

## 7. Quality Plans and University Purpose

Examination of university quality plans show that although universities express their overarching mission and goals in terms of diverse educational purposes, the pressure for performance indicators has forced universities to express their measures of success in the language of business. This centralises a small number of the traditional concerns of universities but marginalises many of the educational aspects of their mission, especially those that are difficult to commodify. Ultimately the adoption of the language of business as the medium to evaluate the success of universities, distorts purposes, roles, and relationships. The quality plans of all five universities were couched in the language of corporate business, when they reported their proposals for evaluating their performance. The methods of measurement contained in the quality plans aligned with the assumption that the students have customer relationships to the university, for example, the naïve use of surveys of student satisfaction, statistics on student retention, and attrition. Universities did not claim that students were their customers, although one university claimed that students and others were its 'clients.'

Three quality indicators were common to all five universities. The tacit assumptions that provide justification for these measures are not mutually consistent. Justification for use of the 'Course Experience Questionnaire,' which measures student satisfaction with their course, is based on the tacit assumption that students are customers. Justification for use of the 'Graduate Destinations Survey,' which is used as a proxy measure of employer satisfaction with graduates and measures the number of graduates obtaining fulltime employment, relies on the tacit assumption that employers are customers and students are products. Justification for the use of the student progress and attrition data, which are used as a measure of efficiency in 'processing' students, is based on the tacit assumption that quality is defined as efficiency and value for money. The validity of underlying assumptions on which measures depend has been inadequately investigated,[64] although the technical consistency of measures has been extensively scrutinised.[65,66,67,68,69,70] Data collection strategies of the five universities focused mainly on verifying the market positioning and competitive advantage of each institution relative to other universities, who were cast as competitors. For example universities indicated how they fared relative to other universities in their ability to attract students, in the competitiveness of entry requirements and in how well they attracted the school leavers with the highest examination scores, and in the public *reputation* that the institution had gained.

A. Analysis of Research Findings

The research findings raise three questions. Do students (or any other entity) have a customer relationship with universities? Can the relationship between students, universities academic staff and society be usefully and legitimately conceptualised in terms of stakeholder relationships and if so, what are the implications of this? Can commercial quality management methods be adapted to incorporate stakeholders in place of customers?

**8.    Customers and Universities**

Commercial quality management assumes there is a customer relationship between the business and the organisation or person who buys their products. Even in commerce, quality management that relies on satisfying customers' wants and needs is problematic in some circumstances, especially when there is high variability in customers wants.[71] Research indicates that student expectations are varied, so the 'private university' with the mission of giving customers what they want might still have some difficulties. In education there is further potential for mismatch between students expectations and the ability of universities to satisfy students. Consider the following example. A student may want credentials that will provide access to a good job,[72] but they may not want a course that will take the time necessary to enable them to succeed, they may not want to put the time and effort into study. They may have a faulty understanding of the means ends linkages between what they want and what they need to do to get what they want. In this case, the university may offer an interesting and appropriate course leading to the desired qualification but the student may be dissatisfied, because they are unwilling or unable to put in the necessary effort needed to meet the requirements. Consider also that student wants may change over time in response to education.[73] Student wants may also be conflicting. What students *want* may not be what they *need* to achieve their self-identified goals, if their knowledge of means ends linkages is inaccurate. Notwithstanding these difficulties, this section of the chapter explores the implications of the concept of customer for the roles and relationships implied by the purposes of higher education. The questions asked include: if students were the customers of universities, what would be the universities' product? Can student customers legitimately determine the standard of the product? What would be the implications for others who consider they have interests in higher education? How would this affect the purposes of higher education? What are the implications for funding and for equity issues? How would this affect the economic purposes of higher education?

If students were customers of universities, what would be the product they purchased? Are students buying a qualification or an educational process with the potential for a qualification at the end? The product cannot be the qualification, as achievement of the qualification depends on ongoing requisite effort on the part of the student. The product must therefore be the curriculum and teaching process. Quentin Scrabec suggested that students cannot have a customer relationship with universities because this would enable them to dictate the standards of the product.[74] This is disputed by Craig Swenson who claims that students can be customers without dictating standards.[75] Although Swenson might be right if universities simply prepared students for awards that were examined entirely independently of the university, in a situation where universities internally examine their students and award degrees sometimes without external moderation (as is the case in Australia) Scrabec is right in believing that in a free market situation, universities would be very tempted to adjust their standards to meet the market. In a market situation where universities were struggling to maintain their own short-term income stream, there would be a grave risk that universities would adjust their standards to suit the short-term requirements of the least engaged students and avoid the unrewarded expense of providing high quality teaching. Finally, if students have a customer relationship with universities, then they cannot also be products and the internal efficiency and priorities of universities are no concern of government.

If students are customers, what legitimate interest do other parties have? If higher education becomes a private transaction between universities and their student customers, no other parties have any legitimate interest. In these circumstances, the public role of universities in society would be minimal, as universities would function as wholly private rather than public institutions. According to market philosophy, both government and business would forgo the right to intervene in university affairs; the provision of higher education would become a private service, paid for by the customer, with no requirements to consider other interests. If students wanted to study subjects that had no obvious societal benefits, this would be their prerogative. The only justifiable government involvement in this scenario would be in consumer protection issues, where the product offered was not as described to the customer. There would be no obligation for education to further social or economic purposes, no need to consider equity issues and no obvious right of government to intervene, except by making private arrangements with potential students to enable them to become customers. Thus, although many parts of government policy would like to convince students that they are customers of universities and therefore should pay for more or perhaps for all of their education, the main thrust of Australian government policy sees universities as drivers of economic growth. This is not compatible with the minimalist concept of university as private institutions.

## 9. Stakeholders and Universities

Recent government policy documents, quality plans of the universities and reports of the AUQA panellists all make assumptions that universities have either multiple 'clients' or multiple stakeholders, (I am not going to examine the implications of a client relationship, which would probably fall between those of a customer and those of a stakeholder and potentially accrues both sets of difficulties). In the literature on the concept of stakeholders in commercial settings, according to Weiss,[76] the following issues emerge: boundary issues concerned with deciding where to draw boundaries between those who have legitimate interests and those who do not; legitimacy issues concerned with what legitimates the idea that persons not directly involved in a commercial relationship have the right to have their interests considered; and difficulty in weighing the conflicting claims between and within stakeholder groups.

A stakeholder approach to relationships between universities and staff, students, industry, government, and the public appears to resolve some of the difficulties arising from the assumption that universities have customers. This section examines some of the implications for accepting a stakeholder model. If universities have a stakeholder relationship with other parties, who would have legitimate claims? How should competing claims be balanced? How would it affect the concept of outputs of universities and the assessment of the nature and standard of the product, output or contribution? How would this affect the purposes of higher education? What would be the implications for funding and for equity issues? Not all these issues can be addressed fully here and the next section will focus on questions of legitimacy and purpose and the implications stakeholder theory for the use of commercial quality management methods.

In higher education, the list of stakeholders usually includes at least students, staff, employers of graduates, clients of consulting services, industry, venture partners, and regional communities.[77] They may also include other interested parties such as professional associations, curriculum developers, accrediting bodies, parents, and education and training bodies.[78] This variation indicates there are unresolved boundary issues concerning who should be considered as a stakeholder. The idea that universities have relationships with a number of stakeholders fits well with the multiple purposes of universities and also with the public interest role of universities, and represents a definite improvement over the suggestion that universities have customers. Andrew Weiss claims that stakeholder theory depends upon "implicit social agreements" to which "all members of society are party."[79] This enables stakeholder theory "to identify and legitimate the interests of stakeholders who are not directly involved, such as communities, who may be affected indirectly as a consequence of the activities of an enterprise."[80] Weiss argues that these implicit social agreements are problematic in the market economy of modern capitalism because they run counter to the existing social contract for business in contemporary society, which he refers to as "the minimalist morality of modern capitalism."[81] The features of stakeholder theory that are problematic in the business world are not problematic in the university context, as long as it is assumed that universities are not operating according to a capitalist market framework.

Problems still remain concerning how the interests of stakeholder groups can be known, whether interests of a single stakeholder group is assumed to be homogeneous, and if they are known how their interests can be effectively pressed within university decision-making. Weiss argues that, in commercial settings, managers traditionally derive their authority from their role as agents of the owner. He argues that Stakeholder Theory makes claims to change the basis of managerial authority away from simply representing the interests of the owner. Whilst in a not-for-profit environment like universities, concern about potential infringement of the rights of owners is not relevant, the problems of increasing managerial power and of determining how conflicting interests should be balanced and represented remain salient for universities in deliberations about how to determine the nature and standards appropriate to university courses, and in determining how courses should be funded and how equity issues should be resolved.

## 10. Customers, Stakeholders and Quality Management

The chapter so far concludes that stakeholder relationships fit with the purposes of higher education better than customer relationships. Two questions remain. Firstly, if universities operate within a market framework, are stakeholder relationships an appropriate description of the relationships between universities, students, society, and government? Secondly, can commercial quality management methods accommodate stakeholders in place of customers? The first question can be answered fairly quickly. The second question requires a longer answer.

For the reasons outlined by Weiss, there are philosophical tensions between stakeholder theory and free market capitalism, because of the moral privilege accorded by market capitalism to rights associated with contract.[82] Market capitalism accords only limited rights to those not immediately party to the contract. This seems to preclude the kinds of claims that stakeholder theory makes that 'communities' or 'the public' have enforceable interests. Thus, if universities operate within a market model and the assumptions of stakeholder theory are incompatible with the assumptions of free market capitalism, stakeholder theory cannot be used to describe the relationships between universities and society. Alternatively, if stakeholder theory applies, then universities cannot be assumed to work within a market framework.

Commercial quality management methods vary in their definitions of quality, but all assume that the relationship between the business and the purchaser is a customer relationship where a customer buys a product. If universities have stakeholders instead of customers then the 'simplifying' benefits of the customer relationship are lost. In applying quality management methods that assume customer relationships it is, in principle, relatively easy to respond to 'customer wants and needs.' When stakeholders are substituted for customers things become more difficult. For example, in the context of universities, if industry wants more engineers, society needs more nurses and students prefer to study law, whose interests should take precedence when universities decide how many student places to offer in different disciplines? If students were customers, the answer would be to expand the law schools. If universities are responsive to stakeholders, then managers, in government departments and in universities must decide the balance of claims and decide the numbers of student places to offer in each discipline.

If quality were defined as 'supporting customer satisfaction in an integrated way' it would be relatively easy to survey customers to find out the extent to which they are satisfied with the service they have received. If students were customers, students would be surveyed. If quality were defined instead as 'supporting stakeholder satisfaction in an integrated way,' there would be no simple way to interpret what this would mean. Consider the example above of the allocation of student places. Suppose a compromise solution were achieved, where extra subsidised student places would be offered in nursing and engineering and universities would be permitted to offer extra places in law but only by charging students full fees. Undoubtedly some students would not get what they wanted. A survey of student satisfaction would perhaps show some students were less satisfied. Engineering and Nursing courses might not fill all their places. If students could not get places in the subjects of their choice, less popular courses may enrol students for whom the course is not their first choice. Some of these students might transfer to other courses if they had the opportunity. The Nursing and Engineering Boards may ultimately be less than fully satisfied with the number or quality of graduates. Employers may not be completely satisfied. In these circumstances data on student attrition and progress and employer satisfaction have no simple relationship to the quality of the courses offered.

Decisions about how student places ought to be allocated are taken by senior managers, but university staff at all levels regularly make decisions that require them to balance competing stakeholder claims. Academic staff choose what tasks to undertake in addition to their basic teaching commitments. Should they devote extra time to student support, should they make time to comment on issues of public interest in the media, should they spend time on research and publication, should they mentor and support other staff or should they contribute to collegial university management processes? In deciding these kinds of priorities staff are making decisions about the relative priority of competing stakeholder claims. The decisions are complex and subjective, much more complex that simply responding to a single customer group, even if within the customer group there are differing expectations.

When there are multiple stakeholders, frequently the wants and needs of some groups must be sacrificed in order to satisfy the wants or need other groups. In universities the basis of such decisions are value-based, contentious, political and contested. Commercial quality management methods are unsuited in circumstances of contested values. Commercial quality management methods assuming customer relationships are therefore unsuited for use in universities.

A. Implications of these research findings

The implications of the research findings for the measurement of quality in universities are that naïve output measures that tacitly assume students are customers or products of universities provide no useful indication of educational quality. The complexity of purpose of universities cannot be usefully reduced to simple indicators. The use of simple indicators privileges small parts of the overall purpose of higher education and risks distorting the overall institutional purpose and operation. The consequence of this is likely to be that only those parts that are measured are prioritised to the detriment of other purposes. The overarching institutional goals will be undermined as staff seek to meet localised targets, by diverting their efforts away from unrewarded tasks.[83]

Lessons from history show that many important ways of understanding the world have been initially perceived as heretical, as for example, the position taken on rationality by philosophers and others during the enlightenment. The heretical perspective in one era can become the transformative perspective in another, and then the orthodoxy against which others rebel at another time. Universities have value as one of the custodians of heretical and transformative ideas in society. To maintain this role some parts of university endeavour must be freed from the requirement to only serve immediate utility. This means that universities will need to continue to have multiple, contradictory and ambiguous purposes. The risk with current measures is that universities will recast themselves as quasi-commercial organisations, readjust their goals accordingly and diminish both their social and transformative purposes. Historically some parts of universities have always had normative and practical functions in the world. Alongside the practical part of the mission of universities, there are benefits in protecting a place for transformative and even heretical perspectives.

## 11. Recommendations and Conclusions

Quality must be conceptualised to take account of the differences between education and commerce. Quality management cannot be based upon methods borrowed from commerce that assume commercial roles and relationships. Methods for quality management in higher education must relate to the full range of purposes of higher education, including the contradictory aspects. Methods able to encompass this level of complexity are unlikely to be tidy, comparable or objective, or amenable to quantitative representation in league tables.

The market model on which quality management is premised marginalises many of the purposes of education, including some that the government seeks to foster. The conception of university as having stakeholders rather than customers, fits better with the purposes of universities, even the more limited range supported within government policy. An acceptance of stakeholder relationships, however, entails a rejection of a market-based model for the function of universities within society and market based commercially derived methods for quality management currently in common use.

## Notes

[1] Anderson, Don, et al., *Quality Assurance and Accreditation in Australian Higher Education: An assessment of Australian and international practice* (Canberra: DETYA., 2000).

[2] Grant Harman and V Lynn Meek, *Repositioning Quality Assurance and Accreditation in Australian Higher Education* (Canberra: DETYA, 2000).

[3] Anderson et al., p5.

[4] Michael Gallagher, *The Emergence of Entrepreneurial Public Universities in Australia, Occasional Paper Series* (Canberra: DETYA., 2000).

[5] Trudi Cooper, "The spectacle of quality in everyday university life: why the emperors have no quality clothes" (Paper read at The Third International Conference of Critical Management Studies Critique and Inclusivity: Opening the Agenda, at Lancaster, UK, 7th -9th July 2003).

[6] Sonya Plowman, *The Centenary of Federation: Australian Prime Ministers from Barton to Howard. Noble Park North* (Victoria: Five Mile Press, 2000).

[7] Anderson, Don, Robert Arthur, and Terry Stokes. 2003. *Qualifications of Australian Academics: Sources and Levels* 1997 [cited 07/05/03 2003]. Available from http://www.detya.gov.au/archive/highered/eippubs/eip97-11/chapter9.htm.

[8] Gallagher, 2000

[9] Candy, Philip C, and Don Maconachie. 2003. *Quality Assurance in Australian Higher Education: A recent history and commentary* 1997 [cited 11/04/2003 2003]. www.avcc.edu.au/policies_activities/quality_assurance/policy/quality_assurance_in_austra.doc.

[10] Marginson, Simon, and Mark Considine. 2000. *The enterprise university: power, governance and reinvention in Australia.* Cambridge ; Melbourne: Cambridge University Press.

[11] Megalogenis, George. 2001. Unchain the nation. *The Weekend Australian*, May 5 -6, 26-27.

[12] Australian Vice-Chancellors' Committee. *The worsening student:teacher ratio* 2001. http:/www.avcc.edu.au/.

[13] Australian Vice-Chancellors' Committee. *The Sources of University Income* 2001. http:/www.avcc.edu.au/.

[14] Gallagher, 2000

[15] Salvaris, M. 2003. *Community and social indicators: How citizens can Measure Progress* 2000 [cited 13/05/03 2003]. http://www.sisr.net/programcsp/published/com_socind.PDF.

[16] DETYA. 2000. MCEETYA's National Protocols for Higher Education Approvals Processes. Canberra: DETYA.

[17] Australian Vice-Chancellors' Committee. *Proposed Australian University Quality Assurance System.* AV-CC, 1 September 1999 http//:www.avcc.edu.au/policies_activities/funding/broad_sectorial_funding/index.htm downloaded 21/03/01.

[18] DETYA. 2000. *The Australian Higher Education Framework.* Vol. 00/G, *Occasional papers*. Canberra: Commonwealth of Australia.

[19] Vidovich, Lesley. 2001. The Chameleon 'Quality': the multiple and contrdictory discourses of 'quality' policy in Australian higher

eucation. *Discourse: studies in the cultural politics of education* 22 (2):249-261.

[20] Preston, David S. 2003. *The Evolution of the English University Mission* 2002 [cited 4th May 2003 http://www.inter-disciplinary.net/ioe1s2.htm.

[21] Levine, Donald N. 2003. *The Idea of University, Take One: On the Genius of this Place*. The Idea of the University Colloquium, November 8, 2000 2000 [cited 20/04/2003 2003]. http://iotu.uchicago.edu/levine.html.

[22] Preston, 2002

[23] Op Cit

[24] Levine, 2000

[25] Pascarella, Ernest T., and Patrick T. Terenzini. 1991. *How college affects student: findings and insights from twenty years of research*. San Francisco: Jossey-Bass.

[26] Levine, 2000

[27] Preston, 2002

[28] Op Cit

[29] Op Cit

[30] Levine, 2000

[31] Boyce, Mary E. 1996. Teaching critically as an act of praxis and resistance. *Electronic Journal of Radical Organisational Theory* 2 (2):1-12.

[32] Preston, 2002

[33] Op Cit

[34] Boyce, 1996

[35] Group of Eight. 2002. *Imperatives and Principles for Policy Reform in Australian Higher Education* 2000 [cited 29 July 2002]. http://www.go8.edu.au/papers/pdfs/2000.08.30.pdf.

[36] Blondal, Sveinbjorn, Simon Field, and Nathalie Girouard. 2003. *Investment in Human Capital Through Post-Compulsory Education and Training: Selected Efficiency and Equity Aspects*. Economics Department Working Paper No 333 2003 [cited 15/05/2003 2003]. http://www.oecd.org/EN/home/0,,EN-home-670-nodirectorate-no-no-no-4,00.html.

[37] Op Cit

[38] Levine, 2000

[39] Alvesson, Mats, and Stanley Deetz. 1996. Critical Theory and Postmodernism Approaches to Organizational Studies. In *Handbook of organization studies*, edited by S. Clegg, W. R. Nord and C. Hardy. London ; Thousand Oaks: Sage Publications.

[40] See for example Claes, Tom. 2003. *"It was not a bad idea...": Defining 'the university'* 2002 [cited 4th May 2003 2003]. Available http://www.inter-disciplinary.net/ioe1s2.htm.
[41] Handy, Charles B. 1988. *Understanding voluntary organisations*. 3rd ed. Harmsworth: Penguin.
[42] McInnis, Craig. *The work roles of academics in Australian Universities* 2000. htpp:/www.deetya.gov.au/highered/eippubs.htm.
[43] Winefield, Tony, Con Stough, Dua Jagdish, and Nicole Gillespie. 2001. The higher education workplace stress survey. Adelaide: University of South Australia.
[44] Cooper, Trudi. 2002. Concepts of 'Quality': and the problem of 'customers', 'products', and purpose in higher education. In Quality Conversations: 2002 Annual International Conference of the Higher Education Research and Development Society of Australasia, edited by A. Goody, J. Herrington and M. Northcote. Canberra: Higher Education Research and Development Society of Australasia.
[45] Walton, Mary. 1989. *The Deming management method*. London: Mercury Books.
[46] Andrews, Les, Phil Aungles, Stephen Baker, and Andrew Sarris. 2001. *Characteristics and performance indicators of higher education institutions, 2000: preliminary report*. DETYA 2000 [cited 19th March 2001]. http://www.detya.gov.au/archive/highered/statistics/characteristics/contents.htmwith.
[47] Candy and Maconachie, 1997
[48] Anderson, Johnson, and Milligan, 2000
[49] National Board of Employment Education and Training. 2003. *The Quality of Higher Education: draft advice* 1992 [cited 11/042003 2003]. http://www.dest.gov.au/nbeet/publications/pdf/92_22.pdf.
[50] Australian Vice-Chancellors Committee. 1992. AV-CC Guidelines for Quality Assurance in University Course Development and Review: Australian Vice-Chancellors Committee.
[51] Vidovich, Lesley. 1998. 'Quality' as accountability in Australian higher education in the 1990's: a policy trajectory. PhD, Division of Social Sciences, Humanities and Education, Murdoch, Perth.
[52] Anderson, Johnson, and Milligan, 2000
[53] Vidovich, 2001
[54] Harman and Meek, 2000
[55] West, Roderick. 1998. *Learning for life: final report*. Canberra: Australian Government Publishing Service.
[56] Kemp, David. 2000. Quality Assured. In *Quality Assurance and Acreditation in Australian Higher Education: a national seminar on future arrangements*, edited by M. Skilbeck and H. Connell. Canberra: DETYA

[57] Kemp, David, 1999. Higher Education: Report for the 1999 to 2001 triennium. DETYA 1999 [cited 19th March 2001]. http://www.detya.gov.au/highered/he_report/1999_2001/loverview.htm.

[58] West, 1998, p12

[59] Op Cit, p46

[60] Kemp, 1999

[61] Nelson, Brendan. 2002. *Higher Education at the Crossroads*. Canberra, Australia: Department of Education, Science and Training, Commonwealth of Australia. p 1

[62] Nelson, 2002

[63] Nelson, Brendan. 2002. *Striving for quality: learning, teaching and scholarship*. Canberra, Australia: Department of Education, Science and Training, Commonwealth of Australia.

[64] Cooper, 2002

[65] McInnis, Craig, Patrick Griffin, Richard James, and Hamish Coates. *Development of the Course Experience Questionnaire (CEQ)* 2001 http:/www.deetya.gov.au/highered/eippubs.htm.

[66] Hand, Terry, and Kerry Trembath. 2001. *The course experience questionnaire symposium*. DETYA 1999 [cited 19/03 2001]. http://www.detya.gov.au/archive/highered/eippubs/99-2/execsum.htm.

[67] Long, Michael , and Trevor Johnson. 1997. Influences on the Course Experience Questionnaire Scales. Canberra: DEETYA.

[68] Guthrie, Bruce. 2002. *Study of Non-Response to the 1996 Graduate Destinations Survey*. DEETYA 1997 [cited 21/01 2002]. http://www.detya.gov.au/archive/highered/eippubs/eip9710/front.htm.

[69] Shah, Chandra, and Gerald Burke. 02. *Student Flows in Australian Higher Education*. Australian Council for Educational Research /Centre for the Economics of Education and Training 1996 [cited 21/01/02]. http://www.dest.gov.au/archive/highered/eippubs/burkeshah/front.htm.

[70] DETYA. *OECD Thematic Review of the First Years of Tertiary Education* 1998 [cited.

[71] Harrison, Michael I, and H. James Harrington. 2000. Service Quality in the Knowledge Age. *Measuring Business Excellence* 4 (4):21-26.

[72] Marton, Ference, Dai Hounsell, and Noel Entwistle. 1997. *The experience of Learning: Implications for Teaching and Studying in Higher Education*. 2nd ed. Edinburgh: Scottish Academic Press.

[73] Op Cit

[74] Scrabec, Quentin, Jr. 2000. A quality education is not customer driven. *Journal of Education for Business* 75 (5):298 -300.

[75] Swenson, Craig. 1998. Customers and Markets: The cuss words of academe. *Change* 30 (5).

[76] Weiss, Andrew R. 1995. Cracks in the Foundations of Stakeholder Theory. *Electronic Journal of Radical Organisational Theory* 1 (1):1-15.
[77] Nelson, 2002
[78] Anderson, Johnson, and Milligan, 2000
[79] Weiss, 1995
[80] Op cit, p 6
[81] Op cit p. 6
[82] Op cit
[83] Sterman, John D., and Nelson Repenning. *Getting Quality the Old-Fashioned Way: Self-Confirming Attributions in the Dynamics of Process Improvement* 1996 [cited.

## Bibliography

Alvesson, Mats, and Stanley Deetz. "Critical Theory and Postmodernism Approaches to Organizational Studies," In *Handbook of organization studies*, edited by S. Clegg, W. R. Nord and C. Hardy. London/ Thousand Oaks: Sage Publications, 1996.

Anderson, Don, Richard Johnson, and Bruce Milligan. *Quality Assurance and Accreditation in Australian Higher Education: An assessment of Australian and international practice.* Canberra: DETYA, 2000.

Anderson, Don, Robert Arthur, and Terry Stokes. *Qualifications of Australian Academics: Sources and Levels 1997* [cited 07/05/03 2003].http://www.detya.gov.au/archive/highered/eippubs/eip97-11/chapter9.htm.

Andrews, Les, Phil Aungles, Stephen Baker, and Andrew Sarris. "Characteristics and performance indicators of higher education institutions, 2000: preliminary report." DETYA 2000
[cited 19th March 2001].
http://www.detya.gov.au/archive/highered/statistics/characteristics/contents.htmwith.

Australian Vice-Chancellors Committee. "AV-CC Guidelines for Quality Assurance in University Course Development and Review." Australian Vice-Chancellors Committee, 1992.

Australian Vice-Chancellors' Committee. "Proposed Australian University Quality Assurance System." AV-CC, 1 September 1999 http//:www.avcc.edu.au/policies_activities/funding/broad_sectorial_funding/index.htm downloaded 21/03/01.

Australian Vice-Chancellors' Committee. "The worsening student:teacher ratio" 2001 http:/www.avcc.edu.au/.

The Sources of University Income 2001 http:/www.avcc.edu.au/.

Blondal, Sveinbjorn, Simon Field, and Nathalie Girouard. 2003. "Investment in Human Capital Through Post-Compulsory Education and Training: Selected Efficiency and Equity Aspects." Economics Department Working Paper No 333 2003 [cited 15/05/2003 2003]. http://www.oecd.org/EN/home/0,,EN-home-670-nodirectorate-no-no-no-4,00.html.

Boyce, Mary E. 1996. Teaching critically as an act of praxis and resistance. Electronic Journal of Radical Organisational Theory 2:2 (1996):1-12.

Candy, Philip C, and Don Maconachie. "Quality Assurance in Australian Higher Education: A recent history and commentary" 1997 [cited 11/04/2003]. http://www.avcc.edu.au/policies_activities/quality_assurance/policy/quality_assurance_in_austra.doc.

Claes, Tom. "It was not a bad idea...": Defining 'the university' "2002 [cited 4th May 2003 2003]. http://www.inter-disciplinary.net/ioe1s2.htm.

Cooper, Trudi. "Concepts of 'Quality': and the problem of 'customers', 'products', and purpose in higher education," In *Quality Conversations: 2002 Annual International Conference of the Higher Education Research and Development Society of Australasia*, edited by A. Goody, J. Herrington and M. Northcote. Canberra: Higher Education Research and Development Society of Australasia, 2002a.

Cooper, Trudi. "Why Student Retention Fails to Assure Quality," In *Quality Conversations: 2002 Annual International Conference of the Higher Education Research and Development Society of Australasia*, edited by A. Goody, J. Herrington and M. Northcote. Canberra: Higher Education Research and Development Society of Australasia, 2002a.

Cooper, Trudi. 2003. "The spectacle of quality in everyday university life: why the emperors have no quality clothes." Paper read at *The Third International Conference of Critical Management Studies Critique and Inclusivity: Opening the Agenda*, at Lancaster, UK, 7th -9th July 2003.

DETYA. *MCEETYA's National Protocols for Higher Education Approvals Processes.* Canberra: DETYA, 2000.

DETYA. *The Australian Higher Education Framework.* Vol. 00/G, Occasional papers. Canberra: Commonwealth of Australia, 2000.

DETYA. *OECD Thematic Review of the First Years of Tertiary Education* 1998.

Gallagher, Michael. The Emergence of Entrepreneurial Public Universities in Australia, Occasional Paper Series. Canberra: DETYA, 2000.

Group of Eight. *Imperatives and Principles for Policy Reform in Australian Higher Education* 2000 [cited 29 July 2002]. http://www.go8.edu.au/papers/pdfs/2000.08.30.pdf.

Guthrie, Bruce. *Study of Non-Response to the 1996 Graduate Destinations Survey.* DEETYA 1997 [cited 21/01 2002]. http://www.detya.gov.au/archive/highered/eippubs/eip9710/front.htm.

Hand, Terry, and Kerry Trembath. 2001. The course experience questionnaire symposium. DETYA 1999 [cited 19/03 2001]. http://www.detya.gov.au/archive/highered/eippubs/99-2/execsum.htm.

Handy, Charles B. *Understanding voluntary organisations.* 3rd ed. Harmsworth: Penguin, 1988.

Harman, Grant, and V Lynn Meek. *Repositioning Quality Assurance and Accreditation in Australian Higher Education.* Canberra: DETYA., 2000.

Harrison, Michael I, and H. James Harrington. "Service Quality in the Knowledge Age," *Measuring Business Excellence* 4:4 (2000):21-26.

Kemp, D. A.. "Quality Assured: a new Australian quality assurance framework for university education"[speech]. DETYA 1999
[cited 19th March 2001].
http://www.detya.gov.au/archive/kemp/dec99/ks101299.htm.

Kemp, David. *Quality Assured. In Quality Assurance and Acreditation in Australian Higher Education: a national seminar on future arrangements*, edited by M. Skilbeck and H. Connell. Canberra: DETYA, 2000.

Kemp, David, "Higher Education: Report for the 1999 to 2001 triennium." DETYA 1999 [cited 19th March 2001]. http//www.detya.gov.au/highered/he_report/1999_2001/loverview.htm

Levine, Donald N. "The Idea of University, Take One: On the Genius of this Place. The Idea of the University Colloquium," November 8, 2000 [cited 20/04/2003]. http://iotu.uchicago.edu/levine.html.

Long, Michael, and Trevor Johnson. 1997. *Influences on the Course Experience Questionnaire Scales.* Canberra: DEETYA.

Marginson, Simon, and Mark Considine. 2000. *The enterprise university : power, governance and reinvention in Australia.* Cambridge ; Melbourne: Cambridge University Press.

Marton, Ference, Dai Hounsell, and Noel Entwistle. *The experience of Learning: Implications for Teaching and Studying in Higher Education.* 2nd ed. Edinburgh: Scottish Academic Press, 1997.

McInnis, Craig, Patrick Griffin, Richard James, and Hamish Coates. "Development of the Course Experience Questionnaire" (CEQ) 2001. http:/www.deetya.gov.au/highered/eippubs.htm.

McInnis, Craig. *The work roles of academics in Australian Universities.* 2000. htpp:/www.deetya.gov.au/highered/eippubs.htm.

Megalogenis, George. "Unchain the nation." *The Weekend Australian*, May 5 -6, (2001). 26-27.
National Board of Employment Education and Training. *The Quality of Higher Education: draft advice 1992* [cited 11/04/2003]. http://www.dest.gov.au/nbeet/publications/pdf/92_22.pdf.
Nelson, Brendan. Higher *Education at the Crossroads*. Canberra, Australia: Department of Education, Science and Training, Commonwealth of Australia, 2002.
———. 2002. *Striving for quality: learning, teaching and scholarship.* Canberra, Australia: Department of Education, Science and Training, Commonwealth of Australia.
Pascarella, Ernest T., and Patrick T. Terenzini. 1991. *How college affects student: findings and insights from twenty years of research*. San Francisco: Jossey-Bass.
Plowman, Sonya. 2000. *The Centenary of Federation: Australian Prime Ministers from Barton to Howard*. Noble Park North, Victoria: Five Mile Press.
Preston, David S. 2003. "The Evolution of the English University Mission" 2002 [cited 04/05/2003]. http://www.inter-disciplinary.net/ioe1s2.htm.
Salvaris, M. 2003. "Community and social indicators: How citizens can Measure Progress" 2000 [cited 13/05/03]. http://www.sisr.net/programcsp/published/com_socind.PDF.
Scrabec, Quentin, Jr. 2000. "A quality education is not customer driven." *Journal of Education for Business* 75 (5):298 -300.
Shah, Chandra, and Gerald Burke. *Student Flows in Australian Higher Education*. Australian Council for Educational Research /Centre for the Economics of Education and Training 1996 [cited 21/01/02 02]. http://www.dest.gov.au/archive/highered/eippubs/burkeshah/front.htm.
Sterman, John D., and Nelson Repenning. "Getting Quality the Old-Fashioned Way: Self-Confirming Attributions" in the *Dynamics of Process Improvement* 1996.
Swenson, Craig. 1998. "Customers and Markets: The cuss words of academe." *Change 30* (5).
Vidovich, Lesley. 1998. " 'Quality' as accountability" in *Australian higher education in the 1990's: a policy trajectory*. PhD, Division of Social Sciences, Humanities and Education, Murdoch, Perth.
Vidovich, Lesley. 2001. "The Chameleon 'Quality': the multiple and contradictory discourses of 'quality' policy" in *Australian higher eucation. Discourse: studies in the cultural politics of education* 22 (2):249-261.
Walton, Mary. 1989. The *Deming management method*. London: Mercury Books.

Weiss, Andrew R. 1995. *Cracks in the Foundations of Stakeholder Theory*. Electronic Journal of Radical Organisational Theory 1 (1):1-15.

West, Roderick. 1998. *Learning for life: executive summary*. Canberra: Australian Government Publishing Service.

West, Roderick. 1998. *Learning for life: final report*. Canberra: Australian Government Publishing Service.

Winefield, Tony, Con Stough, Dua Jagdish, and Nicole Gillespie. 2001.*The higher education workplace stress survey*. Adelaide: University of South Australia.

# CHAPTER NINE

## "A Plea for the Highlands of Scotland": University Reform in the Early Twentieth Century

### Christine D. Myers

**Abstract**
One of the leading proponents of reform in British education in the early twentieth century was Hugh Gunn. A well-travelled educationalist, Gunn saw the need for improvements after spending time in other parts of the Empire and in America. This paper examines Gunn's seminal work (published in 1931) on the Scottish university system which detailed the need for better distribution of universities in Britain brought on by population growth, the desire for convenience, and a desire to reduce class differences in the British educational system at the time. I focus primarily on what Gunn terms "A Plea for the Highlands of Scotland" because in this area of Britain there was a complete lack of higher education, making it impossible for a large segment of the population to advance themselves in society generally. I do this by placing particular emphasis on Gunn's most intriguing position – bilingual education – which he felt was necessary in order to preserve Gaelic culture and stem emigration from Scotland. Other topics I will discuss include the impact of World War I and the Empire on British higher education, and curriculum innovations that have only become part of university study seven decades after Gunn's work.

Key Words: Culture; Empire; Gaelic; Gunn; Highland; Higher education; Reform; Scotland/Scottish; UHI; University.

1. **Introduction**

In January 1931, shortly before his death, Scottish educationalist Hugh Gunn published his book *The Distribution of University Centres in Britain: A Plea for the Highlands of Scotland*. The book outlined the key issues faced by British universities at a time of social and political upheaval, as well as addressing the specific needs of the "benighted Scottish highlands," as Gunn termed them.[1] Gunn based his conclusions on his extensive knowledge of educational systems throughout the British Empire and in the United States, having previously worked and taken degrees in Australia, Scotland, and South Africa, as well as having worked with the Department of Romance Languages at Columbia University in New York City. Hugh Gunn was so thoroughly interested in the progress of universities in Britain that he visited each of them personally in preparation for his early career in Australia.² His comparative approach to the state of British universities in the inter-war period enabled him to not only show what is good about the British systems, but also where they could be improved. In *University Centres* he divided his conclusions into fifteen separate "reasons or considerations for a University in the Highlands."³ For the purposes of this chapter I will be focusing on the key areas of geography, bilingualism, and the exploitation of untapped Imperial resources will be highlighted as they relate to Gunn's plan and the modern situation of university education in the Scottish Highlands.

## 2. Dispersion and Quality of British Universities.

The most basic issue Gunn raised in his book is that of geography or, more specifically, population distribution in Scotland, and the distance of that population from their universities. He noted that in the southern third of Scotland, citizens were all considered close enough to "the present English ideal of being within thirty miles" of a university. The same did not hold true for the Highlands, however, where all the major population centres (Inverness, Oban, Wick and Thurso) are more than 150 miles from such an institution, with Hebridean locations like Portree and Stornoway being further than that.⁴ The distance concern was then compounded by the increase in students attending the existing four Scottish universities of the day. Edinburgh and Glasgow were particularly "overloaded and engorged", with more than four and five thousand matriculated students respectively at the time.⁵ This new influx of students was attributed to the admission of women to the institutions (as legislated by Parliament in 1889) and the increased desire of young people to attain degrees as a means of serving their country and Empire in the wake of the First World War.⁶

The impact of the First World War, and its aftermath, was a pivotal supporting theme in *University Centres*. Despite Gunn's criticism of the British university systems, he was also quick to assert British pride in their universities: "Our British Universities are as good as any, and this was proved during the war."⁷ For the strength of the system to be maintained, Gunn pointed to the existence of locally based universities in Wales, Ireland, and "the great midland cities" that started their own institutions to educate their own people.⁸ This "civic spirit" helped to win the Great War, and while the knowledge of a second conflict was certainly not apparent, the need of the Empire for the best-trained men and women was undeniable in Gunn's mind.⁹ Despite approving of all these new university students, Gunn felt that the Scottish system was simply incapable of keeping up with the demand, nor should it attempt to.

The quality of Scottish higher education was seen to be slipping as professors and lecturers were required to limit personal contact with students in the interests of time, replacing such teaching with "purely examining activities."[10] He in no way accused the faculty or administration of failing in their efforts to provide a quality education for students, but he acknowledged the fact that "it is the excess of numbers that creates the difficulty; the task of the teacher becomes impossible."[11] Gunn believed that the faculty had no other option but to begin "spoon-feeding" information to students in smaller and smaller quantities because there was no time for more in depth study.[12]

This problem was not limited to Scotland. Gunn pointed out that "England and many American and Dominion Universities" had the same ailments, and he gave statistical evidence of over-crowding at Oxford and Cambridge, and especially at the University of London, saying that all of these institutions were suffering from an "excess of numbers."[13] In all of these institutions the students were left to find their own path to education and enlightenment because the faculty were unable to meet the needs of so many. And though this may produce self-reliance, Gunn advocated the need for reform of the system that would enable all the participants in it to succeed to the best of their ability.

In addition to questions of over-crowding, Gunn was worried that the diminished state of university teaching in Scotland had far-reaching effects. The quality of the Scottish system, while of the utmost importance in Scotland, was also of interest elsewhere in the world. He argued that the Scottish system was the one primarily adopted in Australia and Canada for use in their universities, while notable attempts had also been made in South Africa to combine the English residential system with the Scottish lecturing system.[14] The ideals of Scottish universities, then, were the ideals of many institutions throughout the world and if the ideals became tarnished, so too would the transmission of knowledge for many generations.

## 3. Higher Education in Scotland.

Scottish pride in their educational system (at all levels of learning) is well documented. Gunn referred to the fact that the "love of learning has always been associated with the name of Scotland."[15] He continued by noting the once commonly held view that Scotland's educational system was particularly democratic in nature:

> Since their establishment the Universities have kept in close touch with the people, and Literature and Learning have never been the exclusive privilege of the wealthy or the aristocracy. This, no doubt, largely explains the innate desire of the Scottish people for education, and the good grounding obtained by Scottish youth stood them in good stead when they went abroad.[16]

Along with wanting the Scottish universities to remain "close" to the people, Gunn also felt that education was the key to the progress of the Empire. The belief that Scotland's system was uniquely egalitarian, which was presented by George Elder Davie in *The Democratic Intellect* in 1961, has been denounced by most educational historians (including, to some extent, Davie himself) but it is important to remember that this sentiment or myth does underlie Hugh Gunn's conclusions. He clearly agreed with Davie's later argument that there was a "distinctive national inheritance" of education in Scotland, which was one of their key contributions to the Empire and to the world.[17]

To this theoretical argument Gunn added more statistical evidence, this time highlighting the number of overseas scholars who chose to attend Scottish rather than English universities. He felt that "Edinburgh can lay claim to being the imperial university of Great Britain and the Empire."[18] In 1927-28 he noted that Oxford had 509 overseas students and Cambridge had 476 while Edinburgh had 653. In terms of Rhodes Scholars, Edinburgh came in first as well with Oxford and Cambridge again following behind. Gunn said there were "nearly 1,000 overseas students attending the four Scottish Universities, sufficient to form a University by themselves."[19] The popularity of the Scottish system had thus become a large cause of its own troubles.

## 4. Comparisons With Other University Systems.

Hugh Gunn's solution to the over-crowding was to establish a new institution based in Inverness (the capital of the Highlands), with satellite or subsidiary units in other Highland communities.[20] He used as his model for this scheme the governmentally funded American universities of Michigan and Wisconsin which have multiple centres throughout their respective states. Though Gunn looked to the United States for a possible structure for his proposed institution, the idea of a federal or multi-campus system was not new to Scotland.[21] In the previous century Parliament had considered the idea of a "National University for Scotland". This proposal, included in the Universities (Scotland) Act of 1858, would have united the five existing institutions of higher education in the country as constituent colleges in a federal system with standard requirements and examinations.[22]

Some educators at the time feared assimilation with the English system or anglicisation of Scottish institutions, while others took the opportunity to sidestep rivalries between universities in order to strengthen the popular perception of Scottish higher education.[23] Though the Commissioners dropped the idea by the early 1860s, the notion of reforming Scottish universities in such a radical manner opened a considerable amount of debate in all quarters. Gunn noted the impact of Parliament's actions on the course of Scottish education, stating that

Scotland was always much in advance of England in general Education, but when legislation came to be passed since the Union of 1707, it has taken second place, and the influence of English educational policy has not always been beneficial to Scotland.[24]

An amount of Scottish nationalism was present in Gunn's statement to be sure but he did do his best to understate the often-damaging effects of legislation on Scotland's progress. As Robert Anderson comments, "tradition was appealed to in order to resist southern innovations which threatened to make education narrower in scope or more constrained by class distinctions."[25] These worries reappear throughout the history of Scottish education, and Hugh Gunn had seen enough evidence of this pattern to warn against succumbing to it in his work.

### 5. The Preservation of Scottish Culture Through Bilingual Education.

Although it may not have been appreciated in Scotland, Parliamentary legislation was a catalyst for reform of Scottish education in both the nineteenth and twentieth centuries. Following the 1858 Act, Parliament once again intervened in 1889 to pass legislation on Scottish universities. The most significant aspect of this reorganisation of the institutions was the admission of women.[26] Legislation affecting schools also had ramifications for the progress of Scotland's universities. The Education (Scotland) Act of 1918 was specifically criticised by Hugh Gunn because it did not do enough to support the teaching of Gaelic in the schools, and it certainly did not provide financial assistance for the same.[27] The support of Gaelic and other particularly Scottish studies was crucial in Gunn's mind, both as a necessary preservation of culture and as a way to keep the Highlands peaceful. In addition, he noted that society "took the general line that English was the working tongue of the country and that the amount of Gaelic necessary was obtained by colloquial use." Without adequate government funding, resources and trained teachers, the language would surely die out.[28]

Hugh Gunn believed that a Highland university was essential as a way to protect Scottish, or more specifically Gaelic, culture both in language and traditions. The "decentralisation" of university centres was a necessary remedy in practical terms, so that quality Scottish education could be provided to all who desired it.[29] The establishment of an additional university in the north of Scotland would help to preserve aspects of Scottish culture and finally bring the Highlanders within the cultured ideal of Britain as a whole. In this sense, the work of such

Victorian groups as the Society for the Propagation of Christian Knowledge (SPCK), who tried to "civilise" the Highlanders and make them acceptable to the rest of the island, would finally be completed by the presence of an institution of higher learning.[30] With the best of intentions, Gunn referred to the common perception of "the barren two-thirds of Scotland" as "almost barbarous" and "savage", thus necessitating a university to improve every aspect of their lives and make them more valuable members of society.[31] Part of Gunn's revised notion of "taming" the Highlands differed greatly from that of the SPCK in that he wished to embrace local culture and language, rather than trying to replace it with English or lowland variations. He focused in particular on the study of Gaelic, which had been encouraged by Queen Victoria, among others, in the establishment of a Chair at the University of Edinburgh.[32] The language, he argued, must be kept alive because it embodies the "fighting spirit" of the people and it also helps to make Scotland a strong and unique country.[33]

The new university should be bilingual in nature, emphasising rather than ignoring the "mixed nationalities" present in the British Isles.[34] Evidence from the 1921 Census showed that 30-60 per cent of Highlanders still spoke Gaelic at the time, but Gunn noted that the use of the language had "been like a shallow lake in the heat of summer, gradually drying up and receding."[35] Much of this evaporation of Gaelic language and culture was the direct result of the governmentally sanctioned suppression of both following the second Jacobite uprising in 1745.[36] Although the treatment of the Highlanders has since been denounced by historians, Hugh Gunn's spin on the situation was that these actions need not be condemned, but that they should and could be rectified by the government of the time supporting his plan for a new institution. Throughout *University Centres* Gunn tried to separate "political or racial feeling" from "the statement of facts." [37] Clearly he felt that the long-standing belief that Scots were often treated as second-class citizens within Britain plays into his work, though his arguments rise above those of politics because he felt that was education's duty to humanity.

Gunn, however, did bring comparative political perspective to the fore in considering bilingualism, arguing that failing to incorporate local Highland culture might lead to continued conflicts between England and Scotland, just as it had between England and Ireland, and between the British and Dutch settlers in South Africa.[38] In his work organising refugee camps in South Africa during the Boer War and then as Director of Education and a member of the Legislative Council in the Orange River Colony, he spent considerable time reorganising "the whole system of national schools" in the country.[39] This first-hand experience reinforced Gunn's long-held belief in bilingual education and it added another dimension as he tried to "sell" his plan to others.

Once again, Gunn was trying to support his case with arguments that he believed would enable every person of power in Britain to understand this new university as being in their own best interests. The new Highland institution would be of benefit to more than just the Highlanders for it would also aid the other Scottish universities which were weighted down by having to educate more than their fair share of students.[40] The government would find it advantageous to have more well-qualified young people to work in service to the Crown. And the educational level in the whole of Britain would rise, keeping it at the forefront internationally. He intended his plan of regional universities to be applied in England and elsewhere in the Empire, aiding the overworked faculty and administrators, and at the same time strengthening Britain's interests by more effectively educating its citizens.

Another point Gunn raised in this regard was that an encouragement of Gaelic language and culture might stem the desire of Highlanders to emigrate, thus maintaining the strength of Britain itself: "depopulation and apathy must be faced with sympathy and courage." [41] The Scottish diaspora, whether it was caused by political strife, famine, or "the call of enterprise and travel", had significantly weakened Scotland in Gunn's opinion. He felt that the effects were considerable, leaving "the remainder of the people more or less impotent and indisposed to claim their rights" in Britain.[42] His concerns were unfortunately validated in the following decade as unemployment in the Scottish Highlands doubled between 1930 and 1936 and as emigration remained a central concern of the government for much of the twentieth century.[43]

While Gunn's assessment of the situation turned out to be prophetic, no connection was made by the government between Highland emigration and the provision of higher education. In his writing there was certainly no indication that Hugh Gunn was an advocate of Scottish independence but he did want the Scots to remain a strong constituent nation within Britain and the British Empire. It was essential that any new institution in the Highlands help to give the people of the region the necessary support and motivation to be productive citizens of the state.

6. **The Impact of World Events on Scottish Universities.**
There was a general feeling in British higher education in the wake of the First World War that universities' primary responsibility was to train "competent national leaders" to guide the country through uncertain times.[44] The topic was the theme in Stanley Baldwin's address on the occasion of his installation as Rector of the University of Glasgow in January 1930. He challenged the students present to think to their role in the "New World":

Now, if I be right in my contention that our national character is the only foundation on which an abiding democracy can be built, and further that on that character more than on the sword depends the permanence of the empire, what can we do, how can we play our part, to prepare ourselves for the testing time of the next century?[45]

Baldwin's assessment of the world's political situation was Anglo-centric and supported by his clear faith in the role of the League of Nations in European politics. He also noted the "general desire for knowledge, and the quest for learning" in Scotland that he knew had long been "a glorious characteristic of your race."[46] The Scottish heritage, then, was a key component in the progress of higher education in the post-war world. Certainly Gunn's own impressions reinforce this wider debate, and he hoped that world events would provide the necessary impetus to bring about reforms in all the British university systems in this regard.

The great contributions of the Highlands, in Gunn's not wholly unbiased opinion, should be rewarded with a new university, which in turn would give all of British university education a renewed energy or "vigour".[47] The strengths of the Highland Scots, particularly within the Empire in military and commercial terms, were undeniably of benefit to the Crown.[48] The standard reference was made to the Highland regiment who held the Thin Red Line at Balaclava, along with the recounting of loss of lives in the First World War (especially in the Navy).[49] As such contributions had been made with insufficient educational provision in the Highlands, Gunn equated an expansion of higher education in the region with a proportionate expansion of Highland activities in the Empire. Job prospects were improving as a result of imperial service in the early twentieth century, creating a demand for better-educated people. Gunn saw this as a window of opportunity for his scheme, knowing that some sort of expansion of British universities was on the horizon.[50]

7.     **Curriculum Innovations.**
The new Highland university would have one final and most significant contribution to make to the British Empire: it would harness untapped resources, both human and environmental.[51] Along with having a strong Department of Education for the training of teachers, it should also focus on Agriculture and Fisheries and be equipped with adequate laboratories and staff.[52] The need for teachers was on the rise in Scotland following the 1918 Education Act.[53] The undeveloped natural resources could then be studied and utilised by local students, who knew them best already, under the supervision of local teachers who could appreciate the needs of the community.[54]

The practicality of these subjects ran contrary to the traditional university curriculum of the day, but Gunn believed this was a benefit. Indeed, one of the underlying messages of *University Centres* is that a new type of university education was needed to bring Scotland (or any other nation) into the modern world. Gunn also felt that courses of a "practical nature" could provide "a check on [the] cloudy intellectual inefficiency" that he felt was commonplace in British universities at the time.[55] This pragmatic approach to education was innovative in the early twentieth century, originating largely in the United States where Gunn spent time late in his career. He applied new methods developed in American institutions to his plan for the Highlands of Scotland, arguing that "research work could be admirably carried out in the calm atmosphere of the North", as long as there were "adequate laboratories and equipment and staff."[56] Gunn called for the advancement of trade, industry, engineering and science, and in particular for the building of bridges and battleships, which were of clear importance in the maintenance of the British Empire.[57]

Gunn understood that "theory and practice go hand in hand" in education and wanted his new university to provide ample opportunities for students to benefit from both.[58] Furthermore, he encouraged not only the attainment of traditional diplomas and certificates but also a certain amount of "self-education and reflection" that might not result in degrees.[59] This additional type of education he felt would encourage as many people as possible to avail themselves of higher learning while at the same time permitting them to study without leaving already established professions. In this way he was building on the existing "great movements in the way of University Extension Lectures, Summer Schools, and Adult Education" that were making valuable contributions to the education of the people.[60] Scotland had been at the forefront of this movement in the late 1700s and a revival of courses had recently begun with the formation in 1927 of the West of Scotland Joint Committee on Adult Education.[61]

Alexander Morgan, a contemporary of Hugh Gunn, wrote in 1933 of the "great possibilities for the advancement of the higher education of adults who can never become full-time students of a University."[62] He and Gunn agreed on both the value of this extra-mural teaching and on the need for the government to assist in the funding of it. Some assistance did come in the form of a Carnegie Trust Fellowship in the early 1930s to help organise adult courses in Edinburgh. This aid, however, did not do enough to supplement the costs of adult education courses that needed to be funded from an institution's ordinary resources.[63]

## 8. Proposal for Starting a University in the Highlands.

Hugh Gunn also devoted time to the financial question in his chapter "How to Start the University". In strictly practical terms, he calculated (in comparison with similar schemes in other countries) that an annual state income of £20,000 and an endowment of state land would be needed to get the Highland university off the ground. At the time Gunn was working with the American Iona Society, a group of expatriate Scots based in New York City, to raise funds to cover the start-up costs of the new institution.[64] Additionally, he new that an Act of Parliament or Charter would be needed to give the university direction and credibility. From there, temporary buildings could be constructed or acquired so that teaching could commence: "There are some branches such as music, practical science and agriculture, and fisheries that could be started without delay."[65] Further courses in the Arts and Education would be added as the money became available.

If the opportunities suggested were made available, the Highlander would then be able to have "a morsel of that ethereal sustenance which has been lavished on England, Wales and Ireland during the last century."[66] Along with the desire for largely intangible intellectual benefits, Hugh Gunn argued that the proposed new university for the Scottish Highlands should be a complete, "normal up-to-date University." It would gain its distinctiveness from the teaching of Gaelic and strong, environmentally based coursework. He knew that the development of this new institution "would not be very rapid", but it was better to begin as soon as possible so that no more time was wasted in the provision of higher education for the Highlands.

## 9. The University of the Highlands and Islands.

Had Hugh Gunn lived more than a month after the publication of his work, and had the world not dissolved into another devastating conflict, perhaps his vision for such an institution would have become a reality much sooner. As it is, the newly formed University of the Highlands and Islands makes great steps towards providing a real structure for Gunn's dream. Officially created by statutory instrument of the Scottish Parliament in April 2001, the University of the Highlands and Islands (or UHI Millennium Institute) is a network of fifteen colleges and research institutions that are coordinated by an Executive Office in Inverness. As its website reports: "This means that our students can share in the educational advantages of a larger institution while benefiting from the personal attention a smaller college can give."[67] The structure and aims of UHI are remarkably similar to those outlined by Hugh Gunn in 1931, and with the increased expansion of higher education in Britain and the new possibilities brought forward by transportation and information technologies, his vision has actually been surpassed.

Supporters of a Highland university were disappointed in 1964 when Stirling was selected as the location for a fifth university for Scotland, but many involved in setting up UHI believe that they may have benefited from a delayed entry into the world of higher education. As Sir Graham Hills, former Principal of Strathclyde University, notes in his 1997 article on the project:

> As in all times of rapid development, there is merit in coming late and avoiding most of the baggage of the past. Given the potential of information technology and computer assisted learning, it seemed wise to 'go for' these enabling technologies and more easily so without the luggage of older attitudes.[68]

And much like Hugh Gunn, Hills advocates using institutions in other countries as models for a new variety of Scottish university. Robin Lingard, first Director of the UHI Project, observes that the "relevant exemplars were first identified in Finland and Norway, though Sir Graham also found analogues in British Columbia and Australia."[69] This enabled UHI to select the most effective teaching and learning approaches for application in their classrooms, discarding those out-dated practices that still hold pride of place in the ancient universities of the country. As Hills puts it, "reform of the British model is near impossible because too many careers, fortunes and past glories are locked up in the status quo."[70] Thus the traditions that make British higher education significant have also been holding it back from further greatness.

*The Distribution of University Centres* was referred to in the preparation of Hills' report and Hugh Gunn is considered one of the "founding fathers" of UHI. There was also a modern awareness that no "region could expect to fulfil its economic potential without a university and...geographical remoteness need be no bar to creating one."[71] The similarities between UHI's structure and that laid out by Gunn exist largely because it is the most logical way to organise a Highland university. The geographical limitations of the 1930s are reduced in the world of the twenty-first century, when UHI includes two locations in the Shetlands in its system. In other respects, UHI is exceeding Hugh Gunn's original proposal. Instead of calling for bilingualism as Gunn did, UHI is incorporating five languages and cultures in their institutional materials.[72] Another parallel between the work of Hugh Gunn and UHI is the resistance each met in "selling" their idea to the government, as the "line from politicians and officials in Edinburgh was that Scotland was already over-provided with universities and that anyone from the Highlands and Islands seeking higher education need travel no further than Aberdeen or Stirling."[73] In the 1930s as well as the 1990s, this argument refused to acknowledge the basic importance of having a university in a region to both attract people to live there and to keep people from leaving, a point central to the proposals of both Hugh Gunn and UHI.

## 10. Conclusion

In 1931 when Gunn published his seminal work on the Scottish higher education system, he made what he termed "reflections and suggestions" on changes he felt were necessary for the betterment of the Scottish people. The book details the need for better distribution of universities in Britain due to population growth, the desire for convenience, and as a result of the class differences that were reinforced by the university system at the time. Gunn's core belief, that better education for all citizens makes for a better society, has become a standard belief in academia, with modern universities throughout the world citing this as one of their primary functions. As an advocate of bilingual education, it is clear that Hugh Gunn's work was far ahead of its time. Beyond this, however, there is still much that can be learned from a thorough study of his comparisons of universities and cultures around the world. Most important, perhaps, is his belief that the most effective way to improve educational opportunity is to learn through comparisons with other nations and heartfelt reflection.

## Notes

[1] Hugh Gunn, *The Distribution of University Centres in Britain: A Plea for the Highlands of Scotland, Some Reflections and Suggestions* (Glasgow: The Airlie Press, 1931), vii, 44. Gunn was a native of Rogart in Sutherland, he attended the University of Aberdeen and later graduated from Edinburgh.

[2] Ibid, viii.

[3] Ibid, 102-109. The categories listed by Gunn are geography, population, position, race, linguistics, religion, martial renown, local culture, education, emigration, university influence, under-representation, modernisation, over-crowding, and the greatness of the Empire.

[4] Ibid, 25-26, 85-86, 90, 102.

[5] Ibid, 27. Gunn cited the figures of matriculated students at Edinburgh to be 4,259 and at Glasgow to be 5,294.

[6] Ibid, 38.

[7] Ibid, 30.

[8] Ibid, 34.

[9] Ibid, 54-55. Scotland "is a country that draws its main sustenance from the land and exports its sons and daughters to the off-

shoots and outposts of the Empire, is that a cause why is should be overlooked in the provision of higher education and prevented from developing along its natural lines with due respect to its traditions, and hereditary genius?"

[10] Ibid, 29.
[11] Ibid, 31.
[12] Ibid, 30.
[13] Ibid, 31.
[14] Ibid, viii, 41, 43. In 1911 Gunn was invited by the Government of Western Australia to help organise the new university being founded at Perth, so much of the Australian adoption of Scottish methods may have to do with his influence. It should also be remembered that Scottish universities were primarily non-residential, which Gunn saw as one of the reasons the Scottish system was so flexible and easily applied to other countries (and why a Highland institution could now be created).
[15] Ibid, 17. See also Helen Corr, "An Exploration into Scottish Education," in *People and Society in Scotland: Volume II, 1830-1914*, eds. W. Hamish Fraser and R. J. Morris (Edinburgh: John Donald Publishers Ltd., 1990), 290-309.
[16] Ibid.
[17] George Elder Davie, *The Democratic Intellect: Scotland and her Universities in the Nineteenth Century* (Edinburgh: Edinburgh University Press, 1961), xvi. See also Robert Anderson, "In Search of the 'Lad of Parts': the Mythical History of Scottish Education," *History Workshop Journal* 19 (Spring 1985), 83-86.
[18] Gunn, 42.
[19] Ibid.
[20] Ibid, 44, 53-54, 85-86. Inverness, Gunn noted, had a population larger than that of Edinburgh or Glasgow when their universities were established, proving that the community was capable of sustaining such an institution. Additional sites would be located in Stornoway, Portree, Tain, Lairg, Wick, Fort William or Oban, and Dunkeld. See also George Edwin Maclean, *Studies in Higher Education in England and Scotland with Suggestions for Universities and Colleges in the United States* (Washington: G.P.O., 1917), 58-59.
[21] Sheldon Rothblatt, "Federal Universities and Multi-Campus Systems: Britain and the United States since the Nineteenth Century," in *Scottish Universities: Distinctiveness and Diversity*, eds. Jennifer J. Carter and Donald J. Witherington (Edinburgh: John Donald Publishers Ltd., 1992), 164-187.
[22] Marischal College and King's College in Aberdeen merged as a result of the 1858 Act, leaving the number of universities in Scotland at four. For more see Donald J. Witherington, "The Idea of a National

University in Scotland, c 1820-c 1870," in *Scottish Universities: Distinctiveness and Diversity*, 40-55.

[23] Anderson, 83.

[24] Gunn, 8.

[25] Anderson, 83.

[26] For a thorough discussion of the 1889 Universities (Scotland) Act see Christine D. Myers, "'Give her the apple and see what comes of it': University Coeducation in Britain and America, c. 1860-1940," (Ph.D. Thesis, University of Strathclyde, 1999), 8-15, 58-66.

[27] Gunn, 60-61, 77-80, 104-105. For information on the Education (Scotland) Act of 1872 see Corr, 291, 294-301 and R. D. Anderson, *Education and the Scottish People, 1750-1918* (Oxford: Clarendon Press, 1995), 165-192.

[28] Ibid, 61-62.

[29] Ibid, 44, 103.

[30] Christopher Harvie, *Scotland and Nationalism: Scottish Society and Politics 1707-1994* (London and New York: Routledge, 1994), 46.

[31] Gunn, 44.

[32] Ibid, 46. Her Majesty gave a "handsome donation" to help establish the position.

[33] Ibid, 48, 104. Religion also factored into this, for the Scottish Highlands were the first site of Christian activity in Britain when St. Columba arrived from Ireland in the sixth century (landing at Iona in 563 A.D.).

[34] Ibid, 57, 103.

[35] Ibid, 57.

[36] Ibid, 7, 57-58. Gunn referred to these actions by the British government as a "policy of hate". See also Harvie, 21, 39, 86, Michael Lynch, *Scotland: A New History* (London: Pimlico, 1992), 303, 306, 328-329, 334-336, and T. M. Devine, *Exploring the Scottish Past: Themes in the History of Scottish Society* (East Lothian: Tuckwell Press, 1995), 137.

[37] Ibid, 58, 91. He described the British Government as "the most liberty-loving in the world irrespective of party."

[38] Ibid, 62-64.

[39] Ibid, vii-viii. Gunn was appointed to the Directorship in 1902 and worked in that capacity until 1910, even representing South Africa at the first Imperial Conference on Education held in London in 1907.

[40] Ibid, 76, 108.

[41] Ibid, 106.

[42] Ibid, 6.

[43] Ewan A. Cameron, "The Scottish Highlands: From Congested District to Objective One," in *Scotland in the 20$^{th}$ Century*, eds. T. M. Devine and R. J. Finlay (Edinburgh: Edinburgh University Press, 1996),

154-157.

[44] Reba N. Soffer, "Modern Universities and National Values 1850-1930," *Historical Research* LX (1987), 174.

[45] Stanley Baldwin, *The New World. Address delivered to the Students of the University of Glasgow on January 20, 1930 On the Occasion of his Installation as Rector* (Glasgow: Jackson, Wylie & Co., 1930), 17.

[46] Ibid, 10.

[47] Gunn, 56 see also Chapter VIII entitled "Gaelic: What to do".

[48] Ibid, 30, 46-47, 103-104. See also Graham Hills, "The University of the Highlands and Islands," in *A Future for Scottish Higher Education*, ed. Ronald Crawford (Glasgow: The Committee of Scottish Higher Education Principals, 1997), 89.

[49] Ibid, 103.

[50] Soffer, 166.

[51] For more on the expansion of higher educational opportunities in Scotland in the twentieth century see Ian J. McDonald, "Untapped Reservoirs of Talent? Social Class and Opportunities in Scottish Higher Education 1910-1960," *Scottish Educational Studies* (1967), 52-58.

[52] Gunn, 43, 83, 97, 107.

[53] Adam Collier, "Social Origins of a Sample of Entrants to Glasgow University," *Sociological Review* XXX (1938), 275.

[54] Gunn, 107-108. He specifically said the university "should assist in exploiting the untapped resources of the North" and this was forty years before the discovery of North Sea Oil!

[55] Ibid, 29.

[56] Ibid, 83. Gunn spent time at Columbia University in New York City working with the Department of Romance Languages in their provision of Gaelic. Always keen to learn about different educational forms in the world, he took the opportunity to study the American system of higher education.

[57] Ibid, 16.

[58] Ibid.

[59] Ibid, 87.

[60] Ibid. Gunn also suggested using "gramophone specialised lessons, wireless or other means" to teach students who were unable to attend traditional courses. Teaching could also be done, in many instances, by local professionals.

[61] Alexander Morgan, *Scottish University Studies* (London: Oxford University Press, 1933), 209.

[62] Ibid, 213.

[63] Ibid, 210, 212.

[64] Gunn, v, xi, 96-97.

[65] Ibid, 97.
[66] Ibid, 109.
[67] "About UHI" UHI Millennium Institute, 2003, (23 September 2003). <http://www.uhi.ac.uk/about/index.shtm>.
[68] Hills, 88, 90. Hills was commissioned to write a report on the prospects for such an institution.
[69] Personal correspondence with Robin Lingard, first Director of the UHI Project from 1992-1996, 8 October 2003.
[70] Hills, 92-93.
[71] Lingard.
[72] See Appendix 1. Note the differences in translation in cultural terms.
[73] Lingard.

## Bibliography

Anderson, R. D. *Education and the Scottish People, 1750-1918*. Oxford: Clarendon Press, 1995.

Anderson, Robert. "In Search of the 'Lad of Parts': the Mythical History of Scottish Education." *History Workshop Journal* 19 (Spring 1985): 82-104.

Baldwin, Stanley. *The New World. Address delivered to the Students of the University of Glasgow on January 20, 1930 On the Occasion of his Installation as Rector*. Glasgow: Jackson, Wylie & Co., 1930.

Cameron, Ewan A. "The Scottish Highlands: From Congested District to Objective One." In *Scotland in the 20$^{th}$ Century*, edited by T. M. Devine and R. J. Finlay, 153-169. Edinburgh: Edinburgh University Press, 1996.

Collier, Adam. "Social Origins of a Sample of Entrants to Glasgow University." *Sociological Review* XXX (1938): 161-277.

Corr, Helen. "An Exploration into Scottish Education." In *People and Society in Scotland: Volume II, 1830-1914*, edited by W. Hamish Fraser and R. J. Morris, 290-309. Edinburgh: John Donald Publishers Ltd., 1990.

Davie, George Elder. *The Democratic Intellect: Scotland and her Universities in the Nineteenth Century*. Edinburgh: Edinburgh University Press, 1961.

Devine, T. M. *Exploring the Scottish Past: Themes in the History of Scottish Society*. East Lothian: Tuckwell Press, 1995.

Gunn, Hugh. *The Distribution of University Centres in Britain: A Plea for the Highlands of Scotland, Some Reflections and Suggestions.* Glasgow: The Airlie Press, 1931.

Harvie, Christopher. *Scotland and Nationalism: Scottish Society and Politics 1707-1994.* London and New York: Routledge, 1994.

Hills, Graham. "The University of the Highlands and Islands." In *A Future for Scottish Higher Education*, edited by Ronald Crawford, 86-96. Glasgow: The Committee of Scottish Higher Education Principals, 1997.

Lynch, Michael. *Scotland: A New History.* London: Pimlico, 1992.

Maclean, George Edwin. *Studies in Higher Education in England and Scotland with Suggestions for Universities and Colleges in the United States.* Washington: G.P.O., 1917.

McDonald, Ian J. "Untapped Reservoirs of Talent? Social Class and Opportunities in Scottish Higher Education 1910-1960." *Scottish Educational Studies* (1967): 52-58.

Morgan, Alexander. *Scottish University Studies.* London: Oxford University Press, 1933.

Myers, Christine D. "'Give her the apple and see what comes of it': University Coeducation in Britain and America, c. 1860-1940." Ph.D. Thesis, University of Strathclyde, 1999.

Rothblatt, Sheldon. "Federal Universities and Multi-Campus Systems: Britain and the United States since the Nineteenth Century." In *Scottish Universities: Distinctiveness and Diversity*, edited by Jennifer J. Carter and Donald J. Witherington, 164-187. Edinburgh: John Donald Publishers Ltd., 1992.

Soffer, Reba N. "Modern Universities and National Values 1850-1930." *Historical Research* LX (1987): 166-187.

Witherington, Donald J. "The Idea of a National University in Scotland, c 1820-c 1870." In *Scottish Universities: Distinctiveness and Diversity*, edited by Jennifer J. Carter and Donald J. Witherington, 40-55. Edinburgh: John Donald Publishers Ltd., 1992.

## Appendix 1

**UHI Mission Statement**
<http://www.uhi.ac.uk/about/uhi_mission.shtm>

In English: To establish for the Highlands and Islands of Scotland a collegiate university which will reach the highest standards and play a pivotal role in our educational, economic, social and cultural development.

In Scots: Ti foond a collegiate university for the Hielands an Islands o Scotland at can growe as guid as the best, an tak foremaist tent to biggin up oor laer an gear, an the fowk an thair tocher.

In Gaelic: Oilthigh colaisdeach a stèidheachadh anns a' Ghàidhealtachd is Eileanan na h-Alba a ruigeas na h-ìrean as àirde agus a chluicheas pàirt chudromach nar leasachadh a-thaobh foghlaim, beò-shlainte, conaltraidh is dualchais.

In Orcadian: All the Colleges in the Highlands and Islands workan together tae mak their own University whar ordinary folk o'all ages can cerry on their schooling tae the highest levels in their own community and celebrating their own wey o'doing.

In Shetlandic: Ta lay up, apo da haemower colleges i da Isles an Hielands o Scotland, a university at will can ta rack da hychest standards, an be a aacht in kyuckerin up wir haemaboot hain, wints an laire.

# CHAPTER TEN

# Funding Challenges for a South African University
# A Case Study

*Herman Rhode and Kirti Menon*

**Abstract:**
The higher education environment both internationally and nationally is on a major transformation trajectory to cope with the need to broaden access, manage knowledge strategically and operate in more cost-effective ways to deal with the reduced resources available for the sector. South African higher education is embarking on a major restructuring exercise aimed at shifting the system from an apartheid-defined landscape to one that is equitable, responsive and improves accessible.

The National Department of Education in South Africa recognises in new plans that funding of higher education is a strategic lever to overcome the inequities of the past. In this chapter, current policy formulations like the new funding formula, the student loan scheme (NSFAS) and financial data of the institution will be examined with a view to extrapolating the intended and unintended consequences of these for the University of the North.

Keywords: South Africa; funding; University of the North; higher education institutions; restructuring.

## 1. The University of the North

The University of the North was established in 1959, as a college linked to the University of South Africa, in terms of the Extension of Universities Education Act No 45 of 1959. An entity created and funded by apartheid, the main purpose of this Bantustan University was to provide black students with sub-standard qualifications in limited fields. The university was traditionally referred to as the radical university, providing education and political training to the current political leadership[1]. Taking together the history and progressive political developments in this country, it was only a matter of time before the university would become one of the melting pots of large-scale political and social dissension, producing ongoing conflict and resultant institutional disruptions.

The period between 1998 and 2001 was particularly turbulent at the university as it teetered on the brink of financial collapse and recorded reduced student numbers with a concomitant effect on the government subsidy received. The institution slid into chaos with major governance problems, which resulted in several changes in management. In 2000 the Minister of Education requested an independent assessor's report on the state of the institution. The report listed 'burning issues' and added "that the institution has been reduced to the level of a bad comedy."[2] The report recommended that the university be shut down for a period of time or that a university Administrator be appointed. In 2001, the Minister dissolved the university council, suspended senior executives and appointed an Administrator whose primary responsibilities were to address the key governance problems and restore stability to the institution.

## 2. Environmental Factors

The present environment in higher education in South Africa places several demands on higher education institutions in terms of compliance with regulatory instruments. It is anticipated that in 2004 a new funding formula will be in place replacing the current funding formula which is largely driven by numbers. Calculated as a percentage of the Gross Domestic Product, Government expenditure on higher education has shifted from 0.77% in 1996/1997 to 0.73% in 2000/2001. It is projected to decline to 0.68% in 2003/2004 in terms of the Medium Term Expenditure Framework.[3]

The Minister of Education has identified the University of the North as an institution to merge with the Medical University of South Africa by 2005. Merger discussions have commenced with the merging partner and these will require further strategic management in order to consolidate the systems developed for normal operations and a semblance of stability.

The Draft Funding Framework released by the Department of Education argues that government should be viewed as the "funder of last resort as far as the higher education system is concerned."[4] The implication is that government will provide funding in relation to government priorities. These proposals in the funding framework are aligned with the sentiment of the White Paper which argues for "goal-oriented, performance-related public funding" of higher education.[5]

It is important to note that, in terms of enrolment trends in higher education, students have been opting for institutions of choice, which very often translates into historically advantaged institutions and a shift to technikons. This shift has impacted student enrolments at historically disadvantaged institutions and has had a corresponding effect on the subsidy allocation from the state.

## 3. Financial Strategy

This case study focuses on the financial management of the institution taking as its departure point the appointment of the

Administrator and the acting Executive Manager of the University of the North in 2001. A decreased state subsidy, an increase in student debtors, and a steep reduction in tuition and residence fee billing confronted the university. Executive management realised that the sustainability of the institution was linked to several major structural issues and systemic deficits that had to be reviewed with urgency. A series of reviews were initiated focusing on the faculty composition of the institution and the service departments of the institution like cleaning, security and horticulture.

Despite the negativity surrounding the university, there were clearly identifiable strengths. The institution provided access to students at an affordable price with facilities for residence, offered qualifications in niche areas like pharmacy, optometry, nursing, teaching and other fields in science and technology and had academic capacity. In the period prior to the appointment of an administrator, academics were in the minority in terms of numbers when compared to support services staff. Students were militant and were not necessarily contributing to the required academic environment. The primary imperative driving management was to gain stability and to ensure the future sustainability of the institution.

Nico Cloete, Ian Bunting and Tembile Kulati provide a typology of institutions in South Africa based on criteria like governance, administration, management capacity and financial stability.[6]

| Type | Traits |
|---|---|
| Entrepreneurial-expanding | • Strong centralised strategic planning, leadership runs institution like business<br>• Cost/business centre financial system<br>• Responsive to student demands and exploring alternative modes of delivery<br>• Attracting other incomes streams |
| Traditional-elite | • Maintenance of postgraduate teaching and research as focus areas<br>• Funding is mainly for research, donor funds<br>• Focus on changing demographic profile of both staff and students<br>• Internal coherence and efficiency as opposed to strong external orientation |
| Stable-emerging | • Strong leadership core<br>• Charting new directions for institution<br>• Experimentation |
| Unstable-uncertain | • Governance problems<br>• Lack of leadership and management capacity<br>• Excellence confined to departments or programmes |
| Crisis-ridden | • Conflict within the governance structures<br>• Poor financial management<br>• Lack of leadership and management capacity<br>• Inability to respond to policy initiatives or market needs |

**Figure 1: Adapted from description in Cloete, Bunting and Kulati**

These categories provide a lens through which to view the status of the University of the North in 2001 and the trajectory of change that accompanied the management practices at the institution to date.

Using the Cloete, Bunting and Kulati typology, it can be stated that the University of the North was crisis-ridden for the period 1999-2000. The optimal goal for management was to incrementally achieve a stable-emerging institution and to effect a shift to the entrepreneurial-expanding type. Management focus for the first phase was to achieve stability and to develop systems to counter the new policies and structural reforms as articulated by the Department of Education.

Management attention focused on setting up valid and functional decision-making structures that would ensure compliance with the regulatory frameworks. There was a consciousness that the finance strategy could not be separated from the overall strategy of the institution in order to maintain a coherent management approach. Executive management identified the areas that posed a significant threat to the institution. These can be listed as:

1) Absence of Council
2) Administrator appointed for an initial period of 6 months as per legislation
3) Suspension of several senior management executives
4) Administrative systems that were not synchronised with the new requirements
5) Reduced capacity at administrative levels
6) High credit risk at the institution
7) Poor public image
8) Reduced student numbers
9) Legal issues inherited from previous administrations

In order to manage the institution, the administrator formed the Interim Advisory Group that served to deal with the executive functioning of the institution and to provide strategic guidance. The Interim Advisory Group was chaired by the Administrator, the Academic Advisor to the Administrator, the Executive Manager of the institution, the Deputy Registrar, the HR consultant, the Legal Advisor, Consultant on Academic Affairs and the Deans of the three newly formed faculties. Meetings were held every week with agendas that covered the functional areas of the institution. The size of the group and frequency of meetings ensured that decision-making was quick, consultative and took into account the impact on other areas of the institution. The holistic approach to management of the institution proved to be effective as issues that were tabled at the meetings ranged from the operational to strategic.

In Phase One, the managers of the institution's finances focused on developing and strengthening the systems, using a top-down approach. A clear list of priorities emerged from the preliminary analysis of the financial status of the institution.

| Operational Financial Issues |
|---|
| Quality of the loan books |
| High cost of operations |
| Skewed proportion of academic vs administrative staff |
| Low income client base |
| Poor retention of students |
| Poor overall throughput rates |
| Irregular cash flows |
| Substantial debt |
| Inappropriate staffing policies |
| Diminished quality of service |
| Lack of capital |
| Inaccurate reporting of data to the Department of Education impacted on funding allocations |

**Figure 2: Operational Financial Issues**

A restructuring plan was prepared which entailed reviewing the academic niche areas of the institution and balancing these against enrolment trends, income streams and the needs of the province. This review resulted in the reduction of faculties from eleven to three, collapsing of departments into eleven schools and the closure of non-productive departments. In addition, audits into service departments resulted in the outsourcing of major non-core areas ranging from horticulture to security. This resulted in massive savings for the institution of approximately R35 million per year, or 18% savings of total salary expenditure. The following table illustrates the impact of the restructuring on staff numbers and the associated effects on salary spend.

| Category of Staff | Before | After |
|---|---|---|
| Academic | 450 | 420 |
| Support | 1200 | 570 |
| Total | 1600 | 990 |

**Figure 3: Number of staff by category**

The media coverage of the University of the North prior to 2001 had focused on the governance problems, financial strain, diminishing student numbers and highlighted the fact that the institution had the highest debt record amongst institutions in the country. The review of the debt record resulted in the discovery that R70 million of the debt remained as a feature of the institution's reports to the Department of Education premised on the false and invalid belief that it would bolster the case for redress funding.

A cash recovery approach was used in setting the tuition and residence fees. By freezing enrolment fees, the institution attracted more students and thereby collected more fees in total. An analysis of recoverable debt and utilisation of collection mechanisms and credit management policies within the institution as well as forging relationships with parents and students resulted in outstanding debtors of a comparatively lower figure of R8.6 million for 2003.

In addition, the university introduced a concerted and co-ordinated recruitment strategy that entailed reviewing admission criteria to niche programmes, attracting high performing students with financial rebate incentives and investing in foundation programmes for under-prepared students. The communication directorate, public relations office and student recruitment administrative centre developed plans for new intakes that took into account public perceptions of the institution and devised systems that were client friendly. This entailed decentralising registration, devolving admissions to faculties and streamlining administrative processes to ensure that students needs could be attended to efficiently. Despite minor resistance to these changes, the institution was able to increase student enrolment figures and ensure that the process was not cumbersome.

In 2001, 110 students were provided with merit awards. This figure increased to 1101 in 2003. Tracking systems were put in place to ensure that they maintained above average academic performance, and a tuition waiver was put in place to ensure that they continued their studies at the institution. This waiver ensured that there was sufficient time for processing of applications for National Student Financial Aid Scheme (NSFAS) loans.

NSFAS was established by government in 1996 to address the issue of increasing student debt yet ensuring the broadening of access to higher education. The National Plan for Higher Education recognises that the NSFAS may require a review of the criteria used for awarding loans as the rising costs of tuition fees are affecting the numbers of awards made annually [3]. It is a valid criticism that, despite the National Plan's plea for massification of higher education, the capacity of the funding resources is limited to accommodate growth. The choices made by students with regard to selection of institutions have impacted the number of student financial aid allocations that an institution like the University of the North can attract. This is borne out by the increase in equity profiles of historically advantaged institutions. The table indicates the decline in NSFAS allocation, as there was no provision made for growth and inflation for 2003.

| Funding Allocations | 2000 | 2001 | 2002 | 2003 |
|---|---|---|---|---|
| Number of Allocations | 3800 | 3318 | 2877 | 4500 |
| Average Allocation in Rand Terms | 7894 | 7846 | 9141 | 4756 |
| NSFAS Allocation in Millions | R30 | R26 | R26.3 | R21.4 |

**Figure 4: NSFAS Funding for University of the North**

The White Paper states that "equity of access must be complemented by a concern for equity of outcomes. Increased access must not lead to a 'revolving door' syndrome for students with high failure and drop-out rates."[3] Analysis of the University of the North's statistics indicated that management's strategy for growth had to be tempered with a focus on quality provision. It was clear that a growth in student numbers was desirable but given the profile of high risk under-prepared students that characterised the student body, the strategy had to focus on the quality of academic programmes on offer. This resulted in an overall focus on academic quality with several initiatives put in place like training of lecturing staff, research methodology workshops for postgraduate students and detailed analysis of student performance data. Deans and Directors of schools were provided with student performance data and guided on processes of review in order to put in place mechanisms to improve performance where necessary. Active interventions from senior management included allocating responsibility to the Research Office to focus on postgraduate supervision and to provide assistance to students that were clogging the system. The financial implications of non-performance of students was highlighted for staff and the required growth and increased throughput of postgraduate students was put forward as an essential component of restoring financial stability to the institution.

The institution's financial strategy was aligned to the proposed introduction of the new funding formula. This proactive approach ensured that the institution would be optimally poised for a formula that focused on student performance and provided greater funding levels for postgraduate students in the fields of science and agriculture which had been identified as niche areas for the institution. An important aspect of planning in the South African higher education system is the Department of Education's approval of programmes and qualifications to be offered by institutions. As part of the planning process institutions have submitted detailed three-year rolling plans identifying niche areas, student enrolment projections, student outputs and outlining plans for proposed new programmes. The Department of Education has provided institutions with a Programme and Qualification Mix for the years 2003-2006 indicating funding approval for an institution. In terms of the proposed new funding formula, the importance of planning for an institution becomes of paramount importance. The institution maintained tuition fees at a constant as benchmarking against other public institutions indicated that the fees were above the acceptable level. It also focused on changing the profile of the student population from low income: high risk to low income: low risk. The improved debt collections systems put in place served to ensure that fees provided a much needed income stream for the institution. In 2002 as a further refinement of the incentive strategy, the institution worked on retention of the high performing students. Students who achieved more than 70% in the previous year of study were given merit awards.

The impact of the above interventions is evident in the increase in full-time equivalent students, which will provide the institution with a corresponding increase in subsidy. The figure below demonstrates the growth in student numbers.

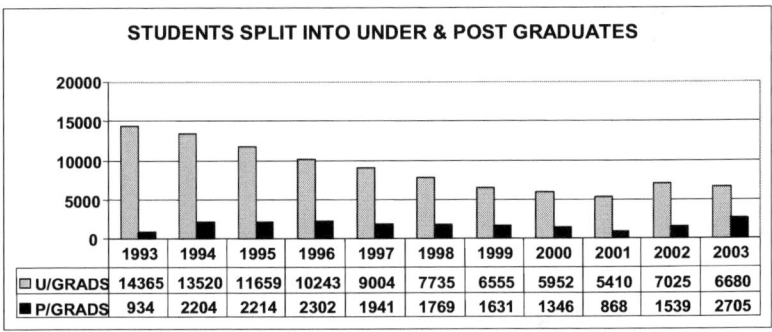

**Figure 5: Growth in Student Numbers**
*2003 figures still to verified.

A critical indicator used by management to determine the success of the above interventions is the anticipated growth in government subsidy. Thus, a demonstrated growth in full-time equivalent students (FTEs) is matched by an increase in the subsidy allocation to the University of the North.

| 2001 | 2002 | 2003 | 2004 | 2005 |
|---|---|---|---|---|
| R155 million | R153 million | R122 million* | R160 million | R180 million |

**Figure 6: Growth in government subsidy**
*The dramatic decline in subsidy stems from the low student enrolment in 2001 (Funding Formula works on n-2)

It must be stressed that the successful turnaround of the institution rested on the premise that reliance on traditional streams of income would not guarantee long-term sustainability of the institution. In tandem with the above interventions, control mechanisms were put in place to reduce operating costs of the institution with minimal impact on the overall quality of teaching and learning. Strategic management planning sessions were held with academics to focus on identifying present income streams, determining the viability status for different programmes and assessing the potential for alternate income streams.

## 4. Conclusion

In 2001, The University of the North relied primarily on the government subsidy, research grants and student fees as sources of income. The management strategy adopted, necessitated reviewing the traditional university model of operations and moving the institution to a more corporate style of operations. This paradigm shift was not easy to effect as the institution is located in a peri-urban area which still carries some of the vestiges of apartheid, and as a result has to fight harder to attract donor funding or even consider more effective use of the plant. Phase Two of the institution's strategic plan is to foster closer working relationships with potential employers, align programme offerings with needs of both the region and the country and increase the employability of the graduates. In order to advance these goals, the university has initiated dialogue with provincial departments and business in the Limpopo region. Some partnerships have been forged between programmes and relevant provincial departments. The successes of these are still to be evaluated. These partnerships and market interactions are unquestionably easier to effect in the urban areas due to the proximity of businesses. Networking and developing the product mix in a rural area brings new challenges and forces the adoption of new and innovative ways of operating.

At this point in time, the institution is immersed in merger discussions as required by the Minister of Education's directives. The anticipated merger in 2005 may derail the institution's ambitions to move to being entrepreneurial-expanding immediately. It has been demonstrated that the adoption of a business-style to the management and linking the institutional strategy to a return on investments model has resulted in the institution emerging as a stable player in the higher education system in South Africa.

## Notes

[1] Philippa Garson, *Academic excellence in the bush.* Weekly Mail & Guardian *15 March 1996* [Available on the internet]
http://www.wits.ac.za/alumni/archive/c_unorth.htm
[2] Focus 20 *A campus farce* 2002
http://www.hsf.org.za/focus20campus.html
[3] Department of Education *The National Plan for Higher Education.* Pretoria 2001b
[4] Department of Education *Funding of Public Higher Education.* Pretoria: 2001a
[5] Department of Education *Education White Paper 3: A Programme for the Transformation of Higher Education.* Pretoria: 1997
[6] Nico Cloete, Tembile Kulati and Mike Phala, *Leadership and Institutional Change in Higher Education.* Centre for Higher Education Transformation and The Tertiary Linkages Project, Pretoria 2000

## Bibliography

Cloete, Nico, Tembile Kulati and Mike Phala, *Leadership and Institutional Change in Higher Education.* Centre for Higher Education Transformation and The Tertiary Linkages Project, Pretoria 2000

Department of Education *Education White Paper 3: A Programme for the Transformation of Higher Education.* (Pretoria: 1997).

Department of Education *Funding of Public Higher Education.* (Pretoria: 2001a).

Department of Education *The National Plan for Higher Education.* (Pretoria: 2001b).

Focus 20, (2002) *A campus farce.*
http://www.hsf.org.za/focus20campus.html

Garson, Philippa. *Academic excellence in the bush.* Weekly Mail & Guardian *15 March 1996* [Available on the internet]
http://www.wits.ac.za/alumni/archive/c_unorth.htm

# CHAPTER ELEVEN

## The Problems Faced By Higher Education Institutions Because of the Constantly Changing Objectives, Sometimes Imposed Externally, Sometimes Self-Imposed

### *Frank McMahon*

**Abstract:**
This paper reviews the extent to which the objectives that universities and other higher education institutions try to achieve are changing and, in particular, how a multiplicity of objectives has emerged. It traces the origin of the sources of pressure for change in objectives and concludes that industry, governments and pan-national organisations all contribute to the development of new objectives. The dependency of universities on external funding makes it impossible to refuse to accept objectives set by governments or other funding agencies. Both the multiplicity of the new objectives and their inconsistency cause difficulties for universities that attempt to achieve them. The paper argues that global trends in higher education are adding to the problems facing university leaders. A possible solution could be found in agreement on a value system that transcends changing objectives but such a value system is not yet in place.

Key words: university; objectives; industry influence; funding; value system.

### 1. Introduction

The role of senior management of all business organisations is to ensure that the organisation achieves the objectives set by the owners/shareholders. This task is simplified if there is but one objective, for example, maximum profit, but the era of multiple objectives has long since arrived. Thus, businesses now try to maximise profit but at the same time try to increase their share of the market, increase the capital value of their shares, behave in an environmentally friendly way, develop new products, etc. This paper addresses the problems which face the leaders of higher education as they strive to achieve objectives which are both multiple and changing.

It is often useful for the reader to know the background and likely prejudices of an author so I will describe myself as male, Irish and one who has worked for the past thirty-three years in higher education. It is I think pertinent to add that only six of those years were as a lecturer, three years as Head of Department and the remainder as Deputy Principal or

Principal/Director. The fact that my role has been primarily managerial has undoubtedly affected my viewpoint. Almost all my work has been in Ireland apart from three years in Zimbabwe and short-term projects in many countries.

There has been concern for some years about the growing complexity of the objectives which universities seek to achieve. Ron Barnett felt (about universities) that "with their competing missions of service, scholarship, military and commercial research, access and income generation, they have no single sense of direction." [1]

If the generation of profit or the maximising of shareholder value provides managers of businesses with a focus for their efforts, there is no agreement on a single objective for universities. Smith and Webster have gone further than bemoaning the lack of an agreed objective and argued that modern universities are "so fractured and differentiated that it may have become absurd to seek to express any grand organizing principle." [2]

All the authors I have quoted above are British but others have expressed similar sentiments, for example the German author Teichler who wondered in 1999 if universities are in danger of becoming "bazaar" universities.[3] And in 1996 I heard Frank Rhodes, former President of Cornell University, set out a litany of complaints made against United States' universities including:

1) neglect of undergraduate teaching by research universities in favour of inconsequential research
2) fragmented fields of study
3) garbled educational purposes
4) trivialised scholarship
5) improper accounting techniques
6) falsification of experimental results
7) conflicts of interest, etc.

He concluded that "universities are perceived as self-indulgent, arrogant and resistant to change". [4]

While noting that Rhodes was well ahead of his time in highlighting problems of improper accounting, I will concentrate on my main point: that the objectives of universities are now perceived as garbled, fractured and without a sense of direction. Since it has been commonly noted that universities are one of very few organisations that have survived for centuries in a recognisable format, it is surprising that a crisis of confidence should have developed in recent years. To analyse the source of this crisis, it is necessary to review briefly the traditional role of the university.

## 2. Role of the University

In the nineteenth century two opposing views of the role of the university were promulgated and influenced the future development of universities. John Henry Newman strongly advocated the teaching role of universities, with a strong emphasis on the benefits of a liberal education in a residential setting. In Germany, Wilhelm von Humboldt emphasised the role of the university in the creation of new knowledge, preferably scientific knowledge. José Ortega y Gasset, a Spanish educational philosopher writing in the 1930s articulated four missions for a university: The Teaching of Learned Professions, Scientific Research, Training for Political Leadership and Creation of Cultured Persons. The Robbins Commission which reported in the UK in 1963 arrived at similar conclusions when it defined four missions for higher education: Instruction in skills; promoting the general powers of the mind; the advancement of learning and the transmission of a common culture and common standards of citizenship.

A decade later the Carnegie Commission of Higher Education proposed five basic functions for American higher education, similar to the Robbins recommendations but introducing the new concept of the enlargement of educational justice for the post-secondary age group. [5]

Thus, in the century between Newman and the Carnegie Commission, the single role of the university -teaching- developed to encompass research and access. But what is more notable about these various definitions of the role of higher education is the absence of any mention of a role in relation to the national, regional or local economy. Neither is there any mention of income generation by universities.

## 3. Higher Education and the Economy

Whilst universities in the UK had enjoyed centuries of autonomy from government control, they came under increased scrutiny during and immediately after the Second World War. The war effort had thrown up shortages of skilled manpower and successive governments looked to the universities to solve these shortages. While universities were financially independent they could ignore requests to modify their in-take of students to satisfy some shortage. But the development of polytechnics and the move to mass education after the publication of the Robbins Report meant that higher education was increasingly dependent on government finance. Such financial aid weakened the independence of the universities (polytechnics never enjoyed the same level of independence), enabling the government to increase its demands on both universities and polytechnics. The introduction of aims related to the economy came via government pronouncements including "The Development of Higher Education into the 1990s" published in 1985. It opined that "The government believes that it is vital for our higher education to contribute more effectively to the improvement of the economy" (paragraph 1.2) and, in an almost threatening manner, "The future health of higher education ... depends significantly on its own success in generating the qualified manpower the country needs" (paragraph. 2.2). This and other government pronouncements altered the environment in which higher education worked in the UK, making it unsurprising that the major review of higher education undertaken by the Dearing Committee in the mid 1990s, should have a different view of the purpose of higher education.

## 4. Dearing Report

The Dearing Report (1997) defined the four main purposes of higher education as being:

1) "to inspire and enable individuals to develop their capabilities to the highest potential levels throughout life, so that they grow intellectually, are well equipped for work, can contribute effectively to society and achieve personal fulfilment;
2) to increase knowledge and understanding for their own sake and to foster their application to the benefit of the economy and society;
3) to serve the needs of an adaptable, sustainable, knowledge-based economy at local, regional and national levels;
4) to play a major role in shaping a democratic, civilised, inclusive society." [6]

When these aims are compared with those outlined by Robbins, the major differences relate to the role of higher education in relation to the economy. Thus, research is no longer justified to merely increase the stock of knowledge but must also be applied to the benefit of the economy. And higher education must serve the needs of the economy at local regional and national levels. Those who lead HEIs must now grapple with reconciling the aims set out above, determining what priorities should prevail as between the development of the student and the demands of the economy.

## 5. Conflicting Aims

Traditionally, universities sought to serve the needs of their students above all other needs, other than an unswerving loyalty to truth. Even in a modern context, one can state this approach in a manner that eschews regional or national loyalties. It was well put by David Teather when he wrote that: "The primary commitment of a university with respect to the pursuit and dissemination of knowledge must be to the world, and not just to the community that gave it birth and supports it"  [7]

But this approach ignores any local, regional or national targets set for the university by the government, quite likely the major provider of funds for the university. It would take a very brave Vice-chancellor to refuse to undertake regional or national initiatives because it was not in the interest of the world community. The loss of funding arising from a principled stand is likely to be unpopular outside the university and may well not withstand internal pressure. Individual faculties and schools within a university pursue sources of funding and are unlikely to appreciate giving up such funding for what some will regard as vague principles. If the pursuit of local and regional agendas is not appropriate for universities, was it appropriate for polytechnics or other institutions of higher education? And if yes, has the abolition of the binary divide in Australia, UK and other countries left a gap for an educational institution geared towards helping the development of the local economy?

There is a discernible trend towards questioning the economic agenda for universities. Roger Scruton's advice written in 2002 could well have been written by Newman:

> Confine learning and teaching within a sacred precinct, shut it off from the world, so that it can move by its own inner force towards futile knowledge and you will produce the whole and healthy mind ..... Relevance is the enemy of knowledge, and when universities make relevance their standard, they betray their mission" [8]

## 6. Changing Definition of a University

The nineteenth century debate about the role of a university seemed to be settled in favour of an institution that encompassed both teaching and research. In recent years it was argued that good teaching needed to be underpinned with research and therefore every self-respecting university had to be engaged in research. This conventional wisdom was under threat from two sources:

(a) Since 1992 and the transformation of UK polytechnics into universities it has been recognised that some universities are much more actively engaged in research than others are. However, this could be attributed to a time factor related to the newness of university status and given time, all the new universities would develop their research activity.

(b) Educational researchers found it impossible to prove that good research resulted in good teaching but often the benefit of the doubt was given, leading to a conclusion that research was an integral part of every university. A good example of this may be found in Barnett and Bjarnason:

It may just be that teaching in the context of research is more likely to produce the inquiring minds which advanced capitalism requires than teaching conducted without that environment.

This cosy consensus on the nature of a university was affronted by the decision of the UK government in June 2003 that universities need not do research. This decision was taken in the context of a decision to allow many teaching institutions to use the university title. There was a hostile reaction from the university community. For once, the vice-chancellors and their staff were united. The former were quoted as saying that breaking the link between teaching and research would devalue degrees and damage the international reputation of UK higher education, while the University teachers were also dismayed: "It makes a mockery of the very concept of a university". [10]

## 7. Industry and Pressure for Change

Whilst it is easy to identify the role of national governments, such as the UK government, in pushing for change, there were and remain other sources seeking change in the same direction. Industry has been a constant critic of practices in higher education, as evidenced by the submissions made to the Dearing Commission. The Institute of Directors expressed strong views to Dearing that "growth in participation seen over the last decade is not compatible with the maintenance of standards" (Dearing p. 37). This is an example of the "more means worse" argument.

The CBI was concerned that the:

> Intellectual demands made on some students (most commonly those of the 1992 universities) may be inadequate and that others (most commonly those of the pre-1992 universities) may not have their generic skills adequately developed. The concerns about standards are greatest in the areas of engineering and science." [11]

Sean Dorgan, CEO of the Industrial Development Authority of Ireland recently called for changes to higher education to advance sustainable competitive advantage and to create strong linkages to business. The address was seen by one commentator as reflecting "the impatience among many in the business community about what they see as the inward-looking nature of Irish education". [12]

In the UK the Chancellor has established the review of links between business and higher education by Richard Lambert, due to report in 2003. Lambert was quoted as saying that "there is a lot of collaboration going on - there has been a step change in the past ten years". [13]

Despite this step change, the Secretary of State for Education still felt that "You have too many employers who think that what is being taught in colleges and universities is not relevant to them". [14]

## 8. International Pressure for Change

European Ministers for Education signed the Bologna Declaration in 1999 setting a number of challenges for higher education in their respective countries including a two-cycle system: an undergraduate cycle of at least 3 years and second cycle leading to Masters/Doctorate. The fact that this system was designed to replace five-year degrees in many European countries, together with the insistence of Ministers that the first cycle award must have relevance in the labour market, leads to suspicions that the move was primarily economic in orientation.

This view is strengthened by the action of the EU in March 2000 in setting the strategic goal to make Europe by 2010 "the most competitive and dynamic knowledge-based economy in the world". To respond to this challenge, the Heads of State and Government agreed some concrete common objectives of education and training systems in Europe, within the overarching principle of lifelong learning with a view to:

1) Improving the quality and effectiveness of education and training systems in the EU;
2) Facilitating the access of all to education and training systems;
3) Opening up education and training systems to the wider world [15]

The European Commission stated the need for excellence in its universities to underpin the knowledge society and achieve the target of Europe becoming the most competitive and dynamic knowledge-based economy in the world. It concluded that European universities are not at present globally competitive and that there were problems in a number of areas. These included the need to enable universities to contribute better to local and regional needs and strategies and the establishment of closer co-operation between universities and enterprises. [16]

The weight of supra-national bodies like the EU behind reform of education should not be under-estimated, not least because the EU has been a major provider of research funding in recent years. In addition, it exerts pressure on member states to join initiatives that are designed to improve the economy of Europe.

## 9. Inconsistent Demands for Change

In the earlier part of this paper I outlined the introduction of new challenges for higher education, principally to aid the economy, both regional and national, and to provide greater access to education. Insofar as these demands are consistently articulated, higher education institutions can gradually take them on board while seeking to safeguard traditional values. But these new demands are not always consistently articulated. A good example of inconsistency can be seen in the New Zealand situation. In the 1990s the government sought excellence by fostering competition between institutions and supported this approach with policies favouring student loans, user pays policies, encouraging international students, and devolution of governance and administration. More recently it has concluded that a new approach based on collaboration and co-ordination rather than competition is appropriate. The criteria of what counts as quality have been extended to embrace equality, citizenship, environmental sustainability and infrastructural provisions. Critical thinking is identified as a key attribute, as is creativity and problem solving and the humanistic ideals of equality, tolerance, care optimism and collaboration. Higher education institutions are expected to take the new policy on board, as the penalty for non-compliance is very clear: their funding will be under threat. "All providers that seek public funds.... will be required to demonstrate both strategic capacity and alignment with national goals." [17]

Similarly in the UK, there has been a re-definition of priorities. In the White Paper published in 2003, Charles Clarke, Secretary of State for Education and Skills identified two areas where universities need to improve:

1) The expansion of higher education to be extended to the talented and best from all backgrounds
2) Need to make better progress in harnessing knowledge to wealth creation ("turn ideas into successful businesses") [18]

He added one additional challenge: He wanted to make the system for supporting students fairer.

## 10. Changing Objectives Under Scrutiny

Most people connected with higher education would describe the movement from an elite to a mass system of higher education as the biggest change of the past thirty years. This move from participation by 10% of the age cohort in higher education to participation by 50% has obviously strained the capacity of managers in institutions to cope. But the problem for those who manage higher education is not just one of coping with a greater number of students. Rather, it embraces meeting the multiplicity of tasks defined by Dearing for UK institutions and similar lists for other countries. Typically, these tasks include teaching an increasing number of undergraduate and postgraduate students, fostering research, promoting social cohesion, co-operating with industry for technology transfer, development of lifelong learning, assisting economic development at local, regional and national levels, raising finance, meeting quality standards and satisfying public accountability. Sir Howard Newby, Chief Executive of HEFCE, felt that the biggest change came from, "the realisation and articulation of the central role of higher education in creating and supporting a modern economy and benefiting society in a wide variety of ways" [19]

While the move towards greater participation in higher education is largely welcomed by most academics, there are fears that the quality of education is suffering. There is simply not enough time to devote to individual students now as there was when class sizes were much smaller. Research into teaching strategies is now addressing ways of overcoming the inherent difficulties associated with growth in numbers.

A second and less obvious problem concerns the control of the curriculum that supports lifelong learning. Richard Pring, Oxford Professor of Education, speaking to the Irish Educational Studies Conference, warned of the danger of the learning society being geared to the goals of economic improvement. Since this agenda is controlled by a relatively small clique with power over qualifications and curriculum, "there is a danger that such a society will work with an impoverished notion of learning." [20]

Other commentators have noted some of the things that have not featured in recent changes in higher education. For example, Barnett *et al* (2001) noted that the undergraduate curriculum has commanded rather less attention than might be expected. Equally, major issues such as being part of the conscience of a democratic system (Dearing) do not figure in the urgings of Western universities. Stephen Rowland found that South African academics strove to create a multicultural society while for British academics the issue was more about the threat caused by market ideology to the social values of co-operation, care and critique.[21] Concern about market ideology also influenced David Preston's exploration of the growth of managerialism, claiming that it is inherently flawed as it is based on achieving the objectives of stakeholders but has no way of quantifying what individual stakes should be. Managerialism has led to the adoption of "the ethic of effectiveness" in which the market is the only judge of whether something is worthwhile and markets are obsessed with measurement of quantity and quality. The need for such measurement has led to a pre-occupation with documentation, auditing and bureaucracy.[22]

It may be true that when one looks back, former times are seen through rose-tinted glasses, leading us to decry what has been lost. This can be illustrated by recounting the story of the Chancellor of the University of Paris who is quoted as "regretting that in the old days.... lectures were more frequent... but now the time taken for lectures is being spent in meetings and discussions". The sentiment is surely familiar but the fact that it was said almost 800 years ago, in 1213, may be surprising.[23]

## 11. Effects of Changing Objectives

Constantly changing objectives, coupled with financial dependency on government finance, has undermined the confidence of managers in higher education. They feel it is necessary to pursue possibilities of extra finance even when it would be better not to do so. Since much of this extra finance comes on a marginal cost basis (rather than full cost) it does not solve the financial dependency of the institution and may even worsen it. Apart from the financial aspect, the pursuit of too many initiatives weakens the focus of the institution and makes the task of managing even more difficult. The extent to which UK universities feel the pressure to earn funding was borne upon me when I recently had luncheon with the vice-chancellor of a British University. He dismissed Foundation Degrees as "rubbish" but followed this by an assertion that if the government provided the money, he would introduce such degrees immediately.

The chief executive of HCFCE sees it as one of the challenges facing his council to change the financial arrangements in a way that discourages the chasing of inappropriate funding.

> Why don't universities currently concentrate on their areas of strength? One answer is that they do but the current funding arrangements may not encourage them to do so sufficiently. A key issue for the Council is how far we can re-engineer our funding model to encourage rather than discourage a greater diversity of mission within the sector. [24]

## 12. Quantifying the Challenge

In this era of benchmarking, we frequently look to the performance of other countries to determine what objectives we should set for ourselves. Ministers for Education often adopt this approach, seeking to identify best practice to guide their own efforts. In this regard, the OECD has been a source of statistical analysis and reports that are very useful to policy makers. I have extracted two tables from Education at a Glance: OECD Indicators, 2002 to illustrate this point. Table 1 shows the educational attainments of the population in age group 25 – 64 years of nine selected countries and the mean for thirty OECD states. Even a cursory glance will reveal major differences in the attainment level of males and females in several countries, prompting the policy maker to ask why and what can be done to redress the situation. Similarly, there are major differences between countries. For example, the attainment of tertiary education is higher in the United States than in any other country and the setting of that level of attainment would be a formidable challenge for many counties.

**Table 1: Percentage Educational Attainment of Population, 2001 in age group 25-64 years, by gender**

|  | Secondary Male | Secondary Female | Tertiary Male | Tertiary Female |
|---|---|---|---|---|
| Australia | 66 | 52 | 27 | 31 |
| Belgium | 59 | 58 | 27 | 28 |
| Denmark | 82 | 79 | 24 | 29 |
| France | 67 | 61 | 27 | 24 |
| Germany | 87 | 78 | 28 | 18 |
| Ireland | 55 | 60 | 35 | 36 |
| Japan | 83 | 83 | 36 | 32 |
| UK | 60 | 57 | 27 | 25 |
| USA | 87 | 88 | 37 | 37 |
| Mean 30 Countries | 66 | 62 | 24 | 22 |

Source: OECD, Education at a Glance OECD Indicators 2002, Paris.
(p. 55)

Table 2 sets out the same data as Table 1 but relates to a narrower segment of the population, age group 25 – 34 years. Because this is a younger age group and one that has benefited from the increased educational opportunities of recent years, one would expect better attainment levels than for the 25 – 64 years age group. This is borne out by the statistics as most countries show a notable improvement in attainment levels. For example, Ireland has surpassed the USA in tertiary level attainment by females, while Japan has achieved the highest completion rate for secondary education.

**Table 2: Percentage Educational Attainment of Population, 2001 in age group 25-34 years, by gender**

|  | Secondary Male | Secondary Female | Tertiary Male | Tertiary Female |
|---|---|---|---|---|
| Australia | 73 | 68 | 29 | 38 |
| Belgium | 74 | 77 | 33 | 39 |
| Denmark | 85 | 88 | 25 | 34 |
| France | 78 | 78 | 32 | 37 |
| Germany | 87 | 84 | 23 | 20 |
| Ireland | 71 | 76 | 45 | 50 |
| Japan | 92 | 95 | 46 | 49 |
| UK | 70 | 65 | 30 | 29 |
| USA | 87 | 89 | 36 | 42 |
| Mean 30 Countries | 73 | 74 | 26 | 29 |

Source: OECD, Education at a Glance OECD Indicators 2002, Paris. (p. 55)

### 13. Some Conclusions

Higher education is in a state of flux as it grapples with the problem of attempting to cope with constantly changing objectives. This problem, difficult in itself, is made worse by the fact that most higher education institutions are heavily dependent on governments for their financial survival. This forces then to do the bidding of their paymasters and to undertake activities that are not in their long-term interest, but which satisfy short-term demands of the government.

As an example of the problem caused by the lack of an agreed mission, one can consider the attitude of universities to improving access to universities by students from groups hitherto under-represented. Governments have in recent years urged universities to take more students from economically and socially disadvantaged backgrounds. Such students may be academically weaker than middle class students from affluent backgrounds, and thus their introduction may have an adverse effect on academic standards achieved. Alternatively, it may be possible to bring disadvantaged students up to the same standards as 'traditional' students but it may require extra resources to do so (more tutorial support, provision of textbooks and a computer, etc.). Thus, the issue of access involves objectives in regard to quality and finance. The absence of agreed objectives makes it impossible to solve this problem, other than by some compromise that may leave no party happy.

We sometimes look to globalisation as a force that may solve some of the world's problems by, for example, increasing the income of individuals and nations. But in the case of higher education, I fear that globalisation may have the effect of worsening the situation rather than improving it. The availability of qualifications through the Internet may place intolerable pressure on traditional providers of education to match the low cost of Internet providers. Since traditional providers do not have the benefit of the economies of scale of Internet providers, they will be faced with unenviable choices of lowering costs (and quality) or pricing themselves out of existence. The current debate on education as a traded commodity and the pressure by large trans-national suppliers (mainly American) to force small countries to remove their barriers to access by global players does not augur well for the future.

A central theme of this paper has been the need for the establishment of a value system, which transcends changing objectives. Such a value system would allow judgements to be made between competing objectives. But in a different context Preston has argued that there cannot be a single consensus view of knowledge. [25] In the more limited field of values that may underpin actions in higher education, I believe consensus can be achieved based on the pre-eminence of the student's welfare. It is important that such agreement is reached and implemented, both nationally and internationally, to avoid continuing unsatisfactory compromises.

## Notes

[1] Ronald Barnett, *The Idea of Higher Education*, (Buckingham: SRHE/ Open University, 1990).

[2] Anthony Smith and Frank Webster, *The Postmodern University?* (Milton Keynes: SRHE/Open University, 1997).

[3] Ulrich Teichler, "Lifelong Learning as challenge for higher education: the state of knowledge and future research tasks," *Higher Education Management*, 11 (1999) 37-53.

[4] Frank Rhodes, "The University: National Powerhouse or Endangered Species?" The Irish Times Lecture, Dublin, 24 September 1996.

[5] Carnegie Commission of Higher Education, *The Purposes and Performance of Higher Education in the United States* (New York: McGraw-Hill, 1973).

[6] National Committee of Inquiry into Higher Education, *Higher Education in the Learning Society (Dearing Report)* (London: HMSO, 1997).

[7] David Teather, *Higher Education in a Post-Binary Era* (London: James Kingsley Publishers, 1999).

[8] Roger Scruton, "The Idea of a University" in *Education! Education! Education!* eds. Stephen Prickett and Patricia Erskine-Hall (Thorverton: Imprint Academic, 2002).

[9] Ronald Barnett and Sava Bjarnason, "The Reform of Higher Education in Britain" in *Higher Education in a Post-Binary Era*, ed. David Teather (London: James Kingsley Publishers, 1999).

[10] John Clare, "Universities need not do research," *Daily Telegraph*, 4 June 2003, p.1.

[11] National Committee of Inquiry into Higher Education, p.37.

[12] Sean Flynn, "Time to rethink Irish education, warns IDA chief," *Irish Times*, 3 March 2003, p. 8.

[13] In an interview in Times Higher Education Supplement, 13 June 2003.

[14] Tony Tysome, "Business will pay if courses meet needs," *Times Higher Education Supplement*, 28 March 2003, p.56.

[15] Commission of the European Communities, *European Benchmarks in Education and Training: follow-up to the Lisbon European Council* (Brussels: European Commission, 2002).

[16] Commission of the European Communities, *The Role of the Universities in the Europe of Knowledge* (Brussels: European Commission, 2003).

[17] Government of New Zealand. *Tertiary Education Strategy 2002 - 2007* (Wellington: Government Printer, 2002).

[18] Dept. of Education and Skills, *The Future of Higher Education* (London: Stationery Office, 2003).

[19] Harold Newby, "The Management of Change in Higher Education," *Higher Education Management and Policy*, 15 (2003): 9-22.

[20] Richard Pring, "A Learning Society, a cautionary note - Presidential Address 1997 Annual Conference," *Irish Educational Studies*, 17(1998): 1-16.

[21] Rowland, Stephen, "Teaching for Democracy," *Teaching in Higher Education,* 8(2003): 89 - 101.

[22] David Preston, "Managerialism and the Post-Enlightenment Crisis of the British University," in *The University of Crisis,* ed. David Preston (Amsterdam: Rodopi. 2002).

[23] Graeme Moodie and Rowland Eustace, *Power and Authority in British Universities* (London: Unwin, 1974).
[24] Harold Newby, "The Management of Change in Higher Education," *Higher Education Management and Policy*, 15(2003): 9-22.
[25] Preston, p. 63.

## Bibliography

Barnett, Ronald. *The Idea of Higher Education*, Buckingham: SRHE and Open University, 1990.
Barnett, Ronald and Sava Bjarnason. "The Reform of Higher Education in Britain" in *Higher Education in a Post-Binary Era*, edited by David Teather, London: James Kingsley Publishers, 1999.
Commission of the European Communities. *European Benchmarks in Education and Training: follow-up to the Lisbon European Council*, Brussels: European Commission, 2002.
Commission of the European Communities. *The Role of the Universities in the Europe of Knowledge*, Brussels: European Commission, 2003.
Dept of Education and Science. *The Development of Higher Education into the 1990s*, London: HMSO, 1985.
Dept. of Education and Skills. *The Future of Higher Education*, London: Stationery Office, 2003.
Government of New Zealand. *Tertiary Education Strategy 2002 - 2007*, Wellington: Government Printer, 2002.
Moodie, Graeme and Rowland Eustace. *Power and Authority in British Universities*, London: Unwin, 1974.
National Committee of Inquiry into Higher Education. *Higher Education in the Learning Society (Dearing Report)*, London, HMSO, 1997.
Newby, Howard. "The Management of Change in Higher Education," *Higher Education Management and Policy*, 15(2003): 9-22.
OECD. *Education at a Glance: OECD Indicators 2002*, Paris: OECD, 2002.
Preston, David. "Managerialism and the Post-Enlightenment Crisis of the British University," in *The University of Crisis,* edited by David Preston, Amsterdam: Rodopi. 2002.
Pring, Richard. "A Learning Society, a cautionary note - Presidential Address 1997 Annual Conference," *Irish Educational Studies,* 17(1998): 1-16.
Rhodes, Frank. "The University: National Powerhouse or Endangered Species?" The Irish Times Lecture, Dublin, 24 September. 1996.

Rowland, Stephen. "Teaching for Democracy," *Teaching in Higher Education,* 8(2003): 89 - 101.

Scruton, Roger. "The Idea of a University" in *Education! Education! Education!* edited by Stephen Prickett and Patricia Erskine-Hall, Thorverton: Imprint Academic, 2002.

Smith, Anthony and Frank Webster. *The Postmodern University?* Milton Keynes: SRHE/Open University, 1997.

Teather, David. *Higher Education in a Post-Binary Era,* London: James Kingsley Publishers, 1999.

Teichler, Ulrich. "Lifelong Learning as challenge for higher education: the state of knowledge and future research tasks," *Higher Education Management,* 11(1999) 37-53.

# Notes on Contributors

**Seth A. Agbo** is currently Assistant Professor of Education and Coordinator of the Education and Learning Program in the College of Education at Pacific University in Oregon. He obtained his Ph.D. in Educational Studies from the University of British Columbia in 1996. He was principal in First Nations schools in Canada and has taught at the State University of New York at Potsdam where he also worked with public schools. His research interests include comparative and international education; the socio-cultural context of education; professional development and teacher effectiveness; community-school relationships; and, lifelong learning and educational policy. He is currently completing a book entitled *Participatory Research, Cultural Literacy and Transformational Learning: Linking Cultures, School Improvement and Professional Development*.

**Denton Anthony** is an Assistant Professor of Business Administration at Saint Francis Xavier University in Antigonish, Nova Scotia. His primary teaching responsibilities are teaching introductory marketing and a senior level course in integrated marketing communications. Denton's primary research interests are in relationship marketing and the role of technology in effective teaching and learning. Denton has presented at several national and international conferences in his research areas including the Academy of Marketing.

**Paramita Atmodiwirjo** teaches architecture at the University of Indonesia. She graduated from the University of Indonesia and is completing her doctoral dissertation at the University of Sheffield. Her major interest is on the relationship between human behaviour and environment.

**Tom Claes** is professor of moral philosophy in the Department of Philosophy and Moral Sciences at Ghent University, Belgium. He teaches courses on twentieth- century Anglo-American metaethics, philosophy of culture, and philosophy of sex. Over the past years he has collaborated in research projects funded by the Flemish Government on the status of the humanities in the university and on the funding structures for scientific research.

**Trudi Cooper** is a Lecturer in the School of International Cultural and Community Studies, at Edith Cowan University, Australia. Before joining Edith Cowan University, Trudi worked in the UK as a Youth and Community Worker, and lecturing in Community and Youth Studies. Her current research interests are quality management in higher education, and the use of portfolio assessment as a means of enhancing learning from professional practice experience.

**Luis Borges Gouveia** has degrees from Fernando Pessoa University (FPU, Portugal) and Lancaster (UK). In the 1990s Dr Gouveia spent five years with IBM as a project manager of Videotex systems. He is currently Assistant Professor at FPU where he is involved in research and development in the use of technology within education. His main interests are in e-learning, information systems and digital cities. In particular he is involved in the conceptualisation of the innovative project of the digital city Gaia Global, involving a region of Portugal with over 300,000 inhabitants.

**Lars K. Hallstrom** is Visiting Assistant Professor of Political Science at St. Francis Xavier University in Antigonish, Canada. He is the author of a number of book chapters and journal articles including, "Environmental Movements in East Central Europe: Between Technocracy and the 'Third Way'" (in *The Politics of Global Arrogance and the Role of Emancipatory Movements*, 2003), "Support for European Federalism? An Elite View" (*Journal of European Integration*, 2003), "Ecology and the State: A Seductive Theory and Limits to Reality" (*International Politics*, 2002), "Learning by Doing: Environmental Attitudes and Participatory Spillover in the 1990s" (*The Journal of the Indiana Academy of the Social Sciences*, 2000), and "Industry vs. Ecology: Environment in the New Europe" (*Futures: The Journal of Economic and Political Forecasting*, 1999).

**Gillian Howie** lectures on philosophy at the University of Liverpool and is director of the Institute for Feminist Theory and Research. She is author of various articles on educational theory, as well as the monograph Deleuze and Spinoza: Aura of Expressionism (Palgrave, 2002). She is currently preparing a work about Adorno and feminism entitled 'Essential Reorientations.'

**Frank McMahon** was born in Dublin, and educated at University College Dublin (B. Comm and MBA). Frank worked for 5 years for a hotel company before taking a job as a Lecturer thirty-three years ago. Since then has worked continuously in higher education, as lecturer, Head of School, Deputy Principal, College Director and currently as Director of Academic Affairs for the Dublin Institute of Technology, Ireland's largest higher education institute. He spent a three year spell as Head of School at Bulawayo Polytechnic, Zimbabwe. At a comparatively late stage, he completed a Doctorate in Education at the University of

Sheffield. He has served as external examiner at six universities (four British, one Ugandan and one Hong Kong) and three Indian institutes, and has twice chaired validation committees for Dutch Polytechnics.

**Kirti Menon** has broad ranging experience in the education sector and more specifically in higher education in the last 5 years. She has extensive expertise in interpretation of policy into implementation frameworks. She has worked as a lecturer and has been a consultant since 1998 to universities, the Council of Higher Education, South African Universities Vice-Chancellors' Association and the Department of Education. For the last two years she has been the Academic Advisor to the University of the North. Ms Menon is a member of the Accreditation Committee for both public and private higher education institutions. She is the Chairperson of the Gandhi Committee.

**Christine D. Myers** is currently a Visiting Assistant Professor of History at Cornell College in Iowa, U.S.A. Her current research interests are in the work of Scottish educationalist Hugh Gunn. In particular Dr Myers is examining the relevance and image of Gunn's ideas in the newly created University of the Highlands and Islands in Scotland.

**David Seth Preston** has degrees from the universities of London, Loughborough and Sheffield. He is currently on the staff of SCoT, London and is Director of the BRG consultancy firm. He is editor of many books and papers including three earlier volumes in this Rodopi series. His interests are in the ethical issues raised by technology. Still recovering from his beloved Middlesbrough winning their first trophy after a wait of 128 years, Dr Preston remains optimistic for a more equitable world. He is married with three children and his main wish for the future is the continued well being of his family. His subsidiary hopes include victory in the 2005 UEFA Cup.

**Herman Rhode** is the Executive Manager of the University of the North in South Africa. He previously held various posts including Director of Finance of the University of the Western Cape. Herman facilitated the transformation of the Committee of University Principals into the South Africa University's Vice Chancellor's Association and established the financial policies and procedures of the Council of Higher Education. He is currently working on a costing analysis for the implementation of the work of the Higher Education Quality Committee.

**Tony Tricker** is professor of Applied Statistics in the Faculty of Arts, Computing, Engineering and Science at Sheffield Hallam University.

He is currently Head of Department of Information Technologies. He has published widely in the field of statistics. His latest research interests are into the methodologies used in the service industries to evaluate 'customer satisfaction.'

**Yandi Andri Yatmo** studied architectural design at the University of Indonesia and the University of Sheffield where he was awarded the Kenneth H. Murta Prize. He has previously been a practising architect in Jakarta and taught architecture at the University of Indonesia. He is currently completing his doctoral dissertation.

# Index

Adorno, Theodor, 19, 26, 27, 34, 35, 188
African diaspora, 49, 51, 59, 63, 66, 67, 68
Australia, v, 115, 116, 117, 121, 125, 131, 133, 134, 136, 137, 138, 139, 141, 143, 151, 153, 175, 181, 182, 187
Barnett, Ronald, 172, 175, 179, 183, 184, 185
Dependency theory, 57
Developing countries, 65
Entrepreneurial University, 71, 74
European Union, 16, 71, 72, 74, 87
Gaelic, v, 141, 145, 146, 147, 150, 155, 158
Gouveia, Luis Borges, i, iii, 37
Gunn, Hugh, v, 141, 142, 143, 144, 145, 146, 147, 148, 149, 150, 151, 152, 153, 154, 155, 157, 189
Higher Education, i, ii, iii, 34, 35, 37, 39, 42, 49, 51, 64, 65, 66, 68, 69, 71, 73, 74, 78, 81, 82, 83, 84, 85, 86, 87, 89, 99, 100, 112, 115, 117, 119, 121, 122, 130, 131, 132, 133, 134, 135, 136, 137, 138, 143, 153, 155, 157, 165, 169, 171, 173, 183, 184, 185, 186, 189
Immigration, 60, 61
Information Society, 38, 40, 42, 73, 85
Lyotard, Jean-Francis, 19, 20, 29, 33, 34, 35
Modernisation theory, 55
Preston, David Seth, vi, 118, 132, 138, 179, 183, 184, 185, 189
Scotland, ii, v, 134, 137, 141, 142, 143, 144, 145, 146, 147, 148, 149, 150, 151, 152, 153, 154, 155, 156, 157, 158, 189
Scottish Highlands, ii, v, 141, 142, 144, 145, 146, 147, 148, 149, 150, 151, 152, 153, 154, 155, 156, 157, 158, 189
Stakeholder, 127, 135, 139
University Fernando Pessoa. Portugal, 44
University of Highlands and Islands, UHI, 141, 145, 148, 150, 151, 156, 158
University of the North, v, 159, 160, 161, 162, 164, 165, 166, 167, 168, 189